Praise for the First Edition of *Dart for Hipsters*

A fun and easy read for anyone wanting to understand what Dart is and how to use it with current generation browsers. The commentary on features planned for future releases of Dart is reason enough to buy this book.

➤ Matt Margolis

At first I was somewhat skeptical of Dart. This book made me understand its promise, gave me a good idea of its current state, and will serve as a solid reference for me to lean on.

➤ Juho Vepsäläinen

This is the first book on this exciting and promising programming language, a clear and approachable text that engages the reader and that certainly will contribute to Dart's success. I particularly liked his treatment of the functional aspects of the language and the discussion of isolates.

➤ Dr. Ivo Balbaert

Dart 1 for Everyone

Fast, Flexible, Structured Code for the Modern Web

Chris Strom

The Pragmatic Bookshelf

Dallas, Texas • Raleigh, North Carolina

Our Pragmatic courses, workshops, and other products can help you and your team create better software and have more fun. For more information, as well as the latest Pragmatic titles, please visit us at *http://pragprog.com*.

The team that produced this book includes:

Michael Swaine (editor)
Potomac Indexing, LLC (indexer)
Liz Welch (copyeditor)
Dave Thomas (typesetter)
Janet Furlow (producer)
Ellie Callahan (support)

For international rights, please contact *rights@pragprog.com*.

Printed in the United States of America.
ISBN-13: 978-1-941222-25-6
Printed on acid-free paper.
Book version: P1.0—October 2014

Contents

Part II — Effective Coding Techniques

Part III — Code Organization

Introduction

Why Dart?

Looking back more than two years to the first edition of this book (really? that long?), I realize that my answer to "why Dart?" has changed. A lot.

I am very much a language, library, and protocol hipster. I love learning new stuff. The fun of learning is very much its own reward, but that is not the main reason that I learn. It is always nice to add another tool to the developer's proverbial toolbox, but I have come to realize even that is not the main driving force to learning.

The main reason that I learn new things like Dart is that I find it to be a most effective way to understand problems from the perspective of others. The folks who write libraries and languages are invariably smarter and/or know the subject matter better than I do, so learning the solutions is a crash course on understanding the problems that currently exist. Even if I cannot use a shiny new tool right away, the challenges faced and overcome by tool authors stick with me.

So, when I first approached Dart, it was very much in that spirit. And wow, did it ever work! I learned a ton from the language and from interacting with people on the mailing list and in blogs. It profoundly affected my way of thinking—not only about languages like JavaScript (which I still love)—but about programming for the Web in general.

That would have been my answer from two years ago. I learn Dart—and I think others should learn it too—because it profoundly affects the way that one thinks about programming for the Web.

But since then...

I have really come to appreciate the intrinsic beauty and value of Dart. More and more, it is my "go to" tool to fulfill important needs. And I love using it.

Dart is not a JavaScript replacement. Let me repeat that: Dart is not meant to replace JavaScript. It is much more. It took me a long while to understand this, but Dart is not a competitor with JavaScript-the-language. It is a competitor with the platform that supports developing JavaScript. And Dart is so far ahead of JavaScript-the-platform that I would consider it a programming mortal sin to use JavaScript when Dart is an option.

I do not hate JavaScript-the-language. Far from it, in fact. Since the first edition of this book, I wrote a *kids* programming book that uses JavaScript to introduce programming to kids. I am not even a closet JavaScript hater who prefers to use "prettier" compile-to-JavaScript languages like CoffeeScript or TypeScript. Even though each of those compile-to-JavaScript languages offers some benefits over pure JavaScript, I like JavaScript enough to code it by itself.

What I do not care for in JavaScript-land is…everything else. Manipulating the DOM is a pain, so we must have a library for that. XMLHttpRequest is ugly, so we need a library for that. Testing is not built in, so a library is needed for that (and test runners and test assertions too!). And a library to manage large codebases. And, of course, we need a library to manage all the libraries. And (some of us) need a library to make JavaScript prettier. And don't even get me started on cross-browser testing, which never does seem to go as planned…

I dislike JavaScript-the-platform because I spend so much time building and maintaining it that I do not focus on what is important: building insanely great applications. With Dart, a consistently beautiful DOM library is built in. HttpRequest, which comes standard with Dart, makes Ajax a breeze. Libraries and packages are included from the outset. Testing is beautiful and easy.

Most importantly, Dart compiles to *cross-browser* JavaScript. Unlike every other compile-to-JavaScript language out there, Dart does not generate JavaScript and hope for the best. It targets a Dart-specific JavaScript compatibility layer that ensures that your crazy animations, visualizations, and effects work everywhere across the modern Web. (Note: The modern Web has a specific meaning for Dart. It is the latest two versions of each of the major browsers: Chrome, Firefox, Safari, Opera, and Internet Explorer. The main reason—some would argue the only reason—*not* to use Dart is when support for old versions of Internet Explorer—9 and lower—is a hard requirement.)

Oh, and did I mention that Dart is a pretty language? Well, it is and it lets you write beautiful, maintainable code.

So my answer to "Why Dart?" has changed. Dart is the ideal language *and* platform for development on the modern Web. It will still profoundly affect how you think. But today it is more. It is the best way to create and maintain insanely great applications on the modern Web.

Who Should Read This Book (Besides Hipsters)?

This book is primarily intended for programmers eager to build rock-solid, cross-browser web applications. JavaScript was originally meant to enhance web pages. It is a testament to Brendan Eich, the inventor of JavaScript, and the resourcefulness of those who followed that JavaScript means so much to the Web. But JavaScript is not built to facilitate rock-solid web applications. Dart has everything needed and more: real modules for organizing large codebases, central package management to enable sharing, cross-browser compatibility, and built-in beautiful testing.

I am also writing for any developer looking to keep their JavaScript skills as fresh as possible. The best way to improve JavaScript skills is through practice and reading other people's code. But sometimes it can radically help to see what the competition is up to. In this case, as we explore what Dart brings to the table, we can better understand the gaps in an admittedly wonderful language.

This book should be of interest to developers learning languages for the sake of learning. I focus quite a bit on the Dart language, especially in those places that it surprised and delighted me.

And of course, hipsters should read this book as well. Dart is just different enough to make it intriguing to the typical language hipster and yet powerful enough to make it worthwhile for the hipster who hopes to change the world.

How the Book Is Organized

I am trying something different with this book. Rather than introducing slices of the language in each chapter, I bite off chunks. Each section starts with an actual Dart project, including some commentary on the choices being made. My goal in these sections is to leverage Dart's avowed familiarity to make significant headway in giving a real feel for what the language is. Since these are real projects, they are great opportunities to point out Dart's strengths and, yes, some of its weaknesses.

Each of these project chapters is followed by smaller, topic-specific chapters that go into a bit more depth about aspects of the language. I use these to cover material that is too detailed for the project chapters and material that cannot be found in current Dart reference material.

So, if you want a quick introduction to the language, you can certainly start by reading the project chapters alone. If you want a more traditional book, then skip the project chapters and read just the topic chapters. Or read it all—I will try to make it worth your time!

The first project is Chapter 1, *Project: Your First Dart Application*, on page 3. Supplementing that project are Chapter 2, *Basic Types*, on page 11; Chapter 3, *Functional Programming in Dart*, on page 21; Chapter 4, *Manipulating the DOM*, on page 29; and Chapter 5, *Dart and JavaScript*, on page 35.

The next project takes the simple Ajax application from *Project: Your First Dart Application* and whips it into something familiar to JavaScript hipsters: an MVC-like code structure. Looking at this in Chapter 6, *Project: MVC in Dart*, on page 45 gives us the chance to really use Dart's fabulous object-oriented programming facilities and leads directly to a more detailed discussion in Chapter 7, *Classes and Objects*, on page 59. And, since no MVC application is complete without events, we talk about them in Chapter 8, *Events and Streams*, on page 77.

If you want to put a language through its paces, extracting code out into a library, especially an MVC library, is a great way to do it. We do just that in Chapter 9, *Project: Extracting Libraries*, on page 85. Following up on the MVC library, we get to talk about Dart's amazing support for libraries and packages in Chapter 10, *Libraries*, on page 93.

Next we'll take a look at dependency injection in Dart with Chapter 11, *Project: Varying Behavior*, on page 103. Unlike JavaScript, Dart is not primarily a dynamic language, though as you'll see in that chapter, it is still possible to perform some tricks of traditional dynamic languages. The follow-up to that project is an introduction to Dart testing, which might just be Dart's killer feature.

The last project chapter is Chapter 13, *Project: An End to Callback Hell*, on page 121, in which we further explore Dart "futures" as a higher-order replacement for traditional callback passing. This leads into a discussion of code isolation and message passing in Chapter 14, *Futures and Isolates*, on page 127.

Finally, we conclude the book with a brief exploration of various HTML5 technologies that are not covered elsewhere in the book.

What Is Not in This Book

We will not cover the Dart Editor. In some regards, this is something of a loss—strongly typed languages like Dart lend themselves to code completion, of which the Dart Editor takes advantage. Still, the focus of the book is meant to be the language, not the tools built around it. Besides, some people (myself included) will want to stick with their code editor of choice.

Although Dart boasts some pretty impressive server-side, Node.js-like features, we will not cover them in this book. Many of the code samples that are included use a web server, so peruse them if you are curious about how that looks.

This book is not intended as a language reference. It has been hard enough keeping even a book this size up-to-date as the language evolves! Still, the hope is that, by being a useful and pragmatic introduction to the language, it can serve as a strong supplement for the API documentation (which is very nicely done).[1]

About the Future

Since Dart continues to evolve, so does this book. Once or twice a year, depending on how quickly Dart changes, the content in this book is reviewed and then revised, removed, or supplemented.

If you identify any mistakes or areas in need of improvement, please record them in the errata: http://pragprog.com/titles/csdart/errata/add. Suggestions for new topics to cover are also welcome!

Conventions

Class names are camel-cased (for example, HipsterModel). Classes have filenames that are identical to the class names (for example, HipsterModel.dart). Variable names are snake-cased (for example, background_color), while functions and methods are lowercase camel-cased (for example, routeToRegExp()).

Let's Get Started

With the preliminaries out of the way, let's get started coding for the Web without the legacy of the Web. Let's code some Dart!

---

1. http://api.dartlang.org

Part I

Getting Started

Dart has a lot going for it, but perhaps the most impressive feature is how familiar it is to programmers with a little JavaScript experience. In these first few chapters, with no previous experience, you'll write a Dart application.

CHAPTER 1

Project: Your First Dart Application

Most programming books start with a "Hello World!" sample. I say, screw that—we're all hipsters here. Let's start coding!

Since Dart is written, above all else, to be familiar, you should not be too far out of your depth diving right in. Let's jump straight to something more fun: an Ajax-powered website. Any true hipster has an extensive collection of comic books (am I right? I'm not the only one, am I?), so let's consider a simple Dart application that manipulates the contents of that collection via a REST-like interface.

At some point, this may prove too much of a whirlwind. Have no fear—we'll go into details in subsequent chapters.

The Back End

Sample code for this chapter can be found in the "your_first_dart_app" branch of https://github.com/eee-c/dart-comics. The back end is written in Dart and requires a few Dart packages to be installed with the Dart pub packagers. Instructions are contained in the project's README.

Being REST-like, the application should support the following:

- GET /comics (return a list of comic books)
- GET /comics/42 (return a single comic book)
- PUT /comics/42 (update a comic book entry)
- POST /comics (create a new comic book in the collection)
- DELETE /comics/42 (delete a comic book)

We won't worry too much about the details of the back end beyond that.

HTML for Dart

Our entire application will follow the grand tradition of recent client-side MVC frameworks. As such, we require only a single web page.

```
your_first_dart_app/web/index.html
<!DOCTYPE html>
<html>
<head>
  <title>Dart Comics</title>
  <link rel="stylesheet" href="/stylesheets/style.css">

  <!-- The main application script -->
  <script src="/scripts/comics.dart" type="application/dart"></script>

  <!-- Force Dartium to start the script engine -->
  <script>
    navigator.webkitStartDart();
  </script>

</head>

<body>
  <h1>Dart Comics</h1>
  <p>Welcome to Dart Comics</p>
  <ul id="comics-list"></ul>
  <p id="add-comic">
    Add a sweet comic to the collection.
  </p>
</body>
</html>
```

Most of that web page should be familiar; it will include simple HTML, links for CSS, and scripts.

HTML Head

The only oddity to note is the first <script> tag, in which *JavaScript* starts the Dart scripting engine.

```
<!-- Force Dartium to start the script engine -->
<script>
  navigator.webkitStartDart();
</script>
```

> **Tip**
>
> Important: As of this writing, it is necessary to kick-start the Dart VM with navigator.webkitStartDart() on Dartium, the Dart-enabled version of Chrome.[1] As you'll see later, there is a Dart package that does this for you.

Next we load the contents of our actual code. The only change here is a different type attribute in the <script> tag, indicating that this is Dart code.

```
<!-- The main application script -->
<script src="/scripts/comics.dart" type="application/dart"></script>
```

There is more to be said about loading libraries and including code with Dart once we reach Chapter 10, *Libraries*, on page 93. For now, it is simply nice to note that loading Dart works exactly as we might expect it to work.

HTML Body

As for the body of the HTML, there is nothing new there, but we ought to note the IDs of two elements to which we will be attaching behaviors.

```
<h1>Dart Comics</h1>
<p>Welcome to Dart Comics</p>
<ul id="comics-list"></ul>
<p id="add-comic">
  Add a sweet comic to the collection.
</p>
```

To the #comics-list UL element, we are going to attach the list of comic books in the back-end data store. We will also attach a form handler to the #add-comic paragraph tag. So, let's get started.

Ajax in Dart

We start our Dart application by loading a couple of Dart libraries with a main() function in scripts/comics.dart.

```
your_first_dart_app/web/scripts/skel.dart
import 'dart:html';
import 'dart:convert';
main() {
  // Do stuff here
}
```

---

1. http://www.dartlang.org/dartium/

As you'll see in Chapter 10, *Libraries*, on page 93, there is a lot of power in those import statements. For now, we can simply think of them as a means for pulling in functionality outside of the core Dart behavior.

All Dart applications use main() as the entry point for execution. Simply writing code and expecting it to run, as we do in JavaScript, will not work here. It might seem C-like at first, but does it honestly make sense that code lines strewn across any number of source files and HTML will all start executing immediately? The main() entry point is more than convention; it is a best practice enforced by the language.

As for the contents of the main() function, we take it piece by piece. We are retrieving a list of comic books in our collection and using that to populate an element on our page.

We need to identify the DOM element to which the list will attach (#comics-list). Next we need an Ajax call to fill in that DOM element. To accomplish both of those things, our first bit of Dart code might look like the following:

your_first_dart_app/web/scripts/comics.dart
```
main() {
  var list_el = document.query('#comics-list');
  var req = new HttpRequest();

}
```

Aside from the obvious omission of the function keyword, this example might be JavaScript code! We will cover more differences in Chapter 3, *Functional Programming in Dart*, on page 21. Still in Dart are the semicolons and curly braces that we know and love—the language designers have certainly made the language at least superficially familiar.

> **Tip**   Note: Unlike in JavaScript, semicolons are not optional in Dart.

In addition to being familiar, this code is easy to read and understand at a glance. There are no weird, legacy DOM methods. We use document.query() for an element rather than document.findByElementId(). And we use the familiar CSS selector of #comics-list, just as we have grown accustomed to in jQuery.

Also note that we are not creating an XMLHttpRequest object. In Dart, it is just HttpRequest. This may seem a trivial change, but remember Dart is written for today's Web, not to support the legacy of the Web. And when was the last time anyone sent XML over web services?

Note: Depending on the version of Dart, the code editor, or tools that you are using, you may see warnings that query() is deprecated. It is not deprecated. Well, not really. The current version is deprecated, but a new query() that behaves nearly identically but tracks newer DOM standards will replace it as soon as the current version is removed. This books opts to future-proof itself by using the current query(), which will work just fine when the new and improved version rolls along. If you really dislike these warnings, feel free to replace instances of query() with querySelector() and to replace queryAll() with querySelectorAll(). The code examples will continue to work just fine.

Tip

So far we have the UL that we want to populate and an HttpRequest object to do so. Let's make the request and, after a successful response, populate that UL. As in JavaScript, we open the request to the appropriate resource (/comics), listen for an event that fires when the request loads, and finally send the request.

```
main() {
  var list_el = document.query('#comics-list');
  var req = new HttpRequest();
  req.open('get', '/comics');
  req.onLoad.listen((req) {
    var list = JSON.decode(req.target.responseText);
    list_el.innerHtml = graphic_novels_template(list);
  });
  req.send();
}
```

Most of that code should be immediately familiar to anyone who has done Ajax coding in the past. We open by creating an XHR object and close by specifying the resource to be retrieved and actually sending the request.

It is when we add event handlers that we see a more fundamental departure from the JavaScript way. The XHR object (er, HR object?) has an onLoad property. The onLoad property is a *stream*. Streams are used everywhere in Dart (server-side, client-side, everywhere) as a means of allowing code to receive data without blocking any other code from executing. In this case, the UI should remain responsive until the data from the HttpRequest is available, at which point we do something with it.

In this case, we parse (well, "decode" in Dart) the supplied JSON into a list of hashes, which might look like this:

```
your_first_dart_app/comics.json
[
  {"title":"Watchmen",
   "author":"Alan Moore",
   "id":1},
  {"title":"V for Vendetta",
   "author":"Alan Moore",
   "id":2},
  {"title":"Sandman",
   "author":"Neil Gaiman",
   "id":3}
]
```

With that, we hit the final piece of our simple Dart application—a template for populating the list of comic books.

```
graphic_novels_template(list) {
  var html = '';
  list.forEach((graphic_novel) {
    html += graphic_novel_template(graphic_novel);
  });
  return html;
}
graphic_novel_template(graphic_novel) {
  return '''
    <li id="${graphic_novel['id']}">
      ${graphic_novel['title']}
      <a href="#" class="delete">[delete]</a>
    </li>''';
}
```

The first function simply iterates over our list of comic books (internally, we hipsters think of them as graphic novels), building up an HTML string.

The second function demonstrates two other Dart features: multiline strings and string interpolation. Multiline strings are identified by three quotes (single or double). Inside the string, we can interpolate values (or even simple expressions) with a dollar sign. For simple variable interpolation, curly braces are optional: $name is the same as ${name}. For more complex interpolation, such as hash lookup, the curly braces are required.

And that's it! We have a fully functional, Ajax-powered web application ready to roll. The assembled code is as follows:

```
import 'dart:html';
import 'dart:convert';

main() {
  var list_el = document.query('#comics-list');
  var req = new HttpRequest();
```

```
    req.open('get', '/comics');
    req.onLoad.listen((req) {
      var list = JSON.decode(req.target.responseText);
      list_el.innerHtml = graphic_novels_template(list);
    });
    req.send();
}

graphic_novels_template(list) {
  var html = '';
  list.forEach((graphic_novel) {
    html += graphic_novel_template(graphic_novel);
  });
  return html;
}
graphic_novel_template(graphic_novel) {
  return '''
    <li id="${graphic_novel['id']}">
      ${graphic_novel['title']}
      <a href="#" class="delete">[delete]</a>
    </li>''';
}
```

And loading the page looks like this:

That is a darned nice start in our exploration of Dart. To be sure, we glossed over a lot of what makes Dart a great language. But in doing so, we have ourselves a very good start on an Ajax-powered web application. Best of all, none of the code that we wrote seemed all that different from JavaScript. Some of the syntax is a little cleaner than what we are used to in JavaScript (no one is going to complain about cleaner code), and those strings are quite nice. But, all in all, it is safe to say that we can be productive with Dart in relatively short order.

This App Won't Run

As written, this application will not actually work anywhere...well, almost anywhere.

Dart is not supported in any browser (not even Chrome). To run this web application natively, we would need to install Dartium—a branch of Chrome that embeds the Dart VM. Dartium is available from the Dart Lang site.[2]

Even after Dart makes it into Chrome proper, we would still be faced with supporting only a subset of browsers on the market. That is just silly.

Fortunately, Dart can be compiled down to JavaScript, meaning that you can have the power of Dart but still target all platforms. To accomplish that easily, we add a small JavaScript library that, upon detecting a browser that does not support Dart, will load the compiled JavaScript equivalent.

your_first_dart_app/web/index_with_js_fallback.html
```
<!-- Enable fallback to Javascript -->
<script src="/scripts/conditional-dart.js"></script>
```

We will discuss that helper file in detail in Chapter 5, *Dart and JavaScript*, on page 35. For now, it is enough to note that our Dart code is not locked into a single browser vendor's world. We are very definitely *not* seeing *The Return of VBScript* here.

What's Next

Admittedly, this has been a whirlwind of an introduction to Dart. It is fantastic to be able to get up and running this quickly. It is even better to feel as though you can be productive at this point.

Still, you're only getting started with Dart, and, make no mistake, your Dart code can be improved. So, let's use the next few chapters to get comfortable with some important concepts in Dart. After that, you'll be ready to convert your Dart application into an MVC approach in Chapter 6, *Project: MVC in Dart*, on page 45.

---

2.   http://www.dartlang.org/dartium/

CHAPTER 2

Basic Types

A recurring theme in this book is that Dart aims to be familiar. If that holds true, then a discourse on basic components of the language should be relatively brief—and it will be. Even so, some introduction to core types can only help. And, naturally, there are a few "gotchas" here and there.

Numbers

Integers and doubles are both number types, which means that both support many of the same methods and operators. Dart numbers work pretty much like they do in many other languages.

primitives/numbers.dart
```
2 + 2;     // 4
2.2 + 2;   // 4.2
2 + 2.2;   // 4.2
2.2 + 2.2; // 4.4
```

As you can see, Dart numbers do "the right thing" when mixing them in operations.

Strings

Strings are immutable, which is a fancy way of saying that string operations create new strings instead of modifying existing strings. Strings (like numbers) are hashable, meaning that unique objects have unique hash codes to tell them apart. If we assign a variable to a variable holding a string, both will have the hash code because they are the same object.

primitives/strings.dart
```
var str1 = "foo",
    str2 = str1;
str1.hashCode; // 596015325
str2.hashCode; // 596015325
```

But if we modify the first string, the result will be an entirely new object while the copy continues to point to the original string.

primitives/string_concat.dart
```
str1 = str1 + "bar";

str1.hashCode; // 961740263
str2.hashCode; // 596015325
```

Dart goes out of its way to make working with strings easy. It is possible to create multiline strings by enclosing them in triple quotes.

primitives/strings_triple.dart
```
"""Line #1
Line #2
Line #3""";
```

In addition to the + string concatenation operator, Dart considers adjacent strings to be concatenated.

primitives/strings_adjacent.dart
```
'foo' ' ' 'bar'; // 'foo bar'
```

This adjacent string convenience even extends to multiline strings.

primitives/strings_adjacent.dart
```
'foo'
' '
'bar'; // 'foo bar'
```

Another convenience of Dart strings is the ability to interpolate variables and expressions into them. Dart uses $ to denote variables to be interpolated.

primitives/strings_interpolation.dart
```
var name = "Bob";

"Howdy, $name"; //  "Howdy, Bob"
```

If there is potential for confusion over where the variable expression ends and the string begins, curly braces can be used with $.

primitives/strings_interpolation.dart
```
var comic_book = new ComicBook("Sandman");

"The very excellent ${comic_book.title}!";
// "The very excellent Sandman!"
```

Multiline strings and built-in expression interpolation are a *huge* win for the beleaguered JavaScripter. This effectively eliminates the need for a separate templating library. Templating is built in!

Booleans

The values true and false are the only allowed Boolean (bool) type in Dart. The notion of "truthiness" does not get simpler than it is in Dart: if it's not true, then it's false. Consider the following:

```
primitives/booleans.dart
var name, greeting;
greeting = name ? "Howdy $name" : "Howdy";
// "Howdy"

/*** Name is still not true ***/
name = "Bob";
greeting = name ? "Howdy $name" : "Howdy";
// "Howdy"

greeting = (name != null) ? "Howdy $name" : "Howdy";
// "Howdy Bob"
```

If you are coming from many other languages, then it will not be a surprise that null, "", and 0 evaluate to false in a Boolean context. It may take some getting used to that "Bob" and 42 evaluate to false as well.

The semantics for truthiness vary slightly in "type-checked" mode (described in *Types*, on page 18), but it is best not to rely on such minor variations. If we always assume that the previous will hold, then we will not get burned.

In Chapter 7, *Classes and Objects*, on page 59, we will explore operator definitions, which allows class-specific definitions of equals / ==. This gives Dart a certain amount of flexibility with regard to Booleans.

Maps (aka Hashes, Associative Arrays)

Key-value pairs are implemented in Dart by Map objects. Defining an options hash creates a Map.[1]

```
primitives/hash_map.dart
var options = {
  'color': 'red',
  'number': 2
};
```

As you'd expect, retrieving values from a Map is done with square brackets.

```
options['number']; // 2
```

---

1. Technically a LinkedHashMap, which is a subclass of Map

Map objects support the usual methods. This includes retrieving keys (the keys getter method) and values (the values getter) and iterating over the entire object with forEach().

```
var options = {
  'color': 'red',
  'number': 2
};

options.forEach((k, v) {
  print("$k: $v");
});
// number: 2
// color: red
```

> **Tip**
>
> The order of key-value pairs is not guaranteed in most classes that implement the Map interface (like Map). Dart includes a LinkedHashMap implementation (in the dart:collection library) that does guarantee iteration in the same order in which key-value pairs are inserted.

One *extremely* useful feature of Map is the putIfAbsent() method. Let's consider optionally adding someone's age to the options Map. To prevent replacing the age if it is already present, we might try something like the following.

primitives/hash_put_if_absent.dart
```
if (!options.containsKey('age')) {
  var dob = DateTime.parse('2000-01-01'),
      now = new DateTime.now();
  options['age'] = now.year - dob.year;
}
```

Hipsters hate conditionals. They are ugly and obscure the intent of our code. What is going on inside the if statement? What is the condition in the if statement? There is no easy way to answer either of those questions without reading the code in detail.

We might try factoring the age calculation out into a separate method to make intent a little clearer. Even that still suffers due to the noise of the conditional.

```
findAge() {
  var dob = DateTime.parse('2000-01-01'),
      now = new DateTime.now();
  return now.year - dob.year;
};
```

```
// weak
if (!options.containsKey('age')) {
  options['age'] = findAge();
}
```

This is where the putIfAbsent() method shines. The following is functionally equivalent to the weaker conditional:

```
findAge() {
  var dob = DateTime.parse('2000-01-01'),
      now = new DateTime.now();
  return now.year - dob.year;
};
```

```
// confident
options.putIfAbsent('age', findAge);
```

That is some clean, hip code. And more important than its inherent hipness is the readability. It makes no difference how long we are away from that code, it will still be patently obvious what it does. putIfAbsent()—learn it, love it. It'll save your life (well, probably not, but it'll make life and code that much sweeter).

Lists (aka Arrays)

Lists of things are a requirement of any language. Easing developers into the language, Dart sticks close to the expected with lists.

```
primitives/lists.dart
var muppets = ['The Count', 'Bert', 'Ernie', 'Snuffleupagus'];
var primes = [1, 2, 3, 5, 7, 11];
// Indexed from zero
muppets[0];     // 'The Count'
primes.length; // 6
```

Dart does provide some nice, *consistent* methods for manipulating lists.

```
var muppets = ['The Count', 'Bert', 'Ernie', 'Snuffleupagus'];

muppets.setRange(1, 3, ['Kermit', 'Oscar']);
// muppets => ['The Count', 'Kermit', 'Oscar', 'Snuffleupagus']

muppets.removeRange(1, 3);
// muppets => ['The Count', 'Snuffleupagus'];

muppets.addAll(['Elmo', 'Cookie Monster']);
// muppets => ['The Count', 'Snuffleupagus', 'Elmo', 'Cookie Monster']
```

There are a number of iterating methods built in as well.

```
primitives/list_iterators.dart
var muppets = ['The Count', 'Bert', 'Ernie', 'Snuffleupagus'];

muppets.forEach((muppet) {
  print("$muppet is a muppet.");
});
// =>
// The Count is a muppet.
// Bert is a muppet.
// Ernie is a muppet.
// Snuffleupagus is a muppet.

muppets.any((muppet) {
  return muppet.startsWith('S');
});
// true

muppets.every((muppet) {
  return muppet.startsWith('S');
});
// false

muppets.where((muppet) {
  return muppet.startsWith('S');
});
// ['Snuffleupagus']
```

Even fold() comes built into Dart. We can use it to count all the letters and spaces that make up the names of our list of muppets.

```
muppets.fold(0, (memo, muppet) {
  return memo + muppet.length;
});
// 31
```

Thankfully, there is not much that needs to be introduced for Dart lists and arrays. They are one of many things in Dart that "just work."

Collections

The iterating methods supported by the List class are defined by Iterable. Any Dart class that behaves this way implements the interface defined by the Iterable class. That consistency throughout the language is extraordinarily liberating—if you know Iterable, you know how to manipulate maps, lists, DOM nodelists, event streams, I/O streams, and more.

There are many members of the Iterable family in Dart. Let's take a quick look at two of them: Set and Queue.

The Set class is an Iterable in which the elements are always unique and that exposes some set operations.

```
primitives/set.dart
var sesame = new Set.from(['Kermit', 'Bert', 'Ernie']);
var muppets = new Set.from(['Piggy', 'Kermit']);
// No effect b/c Ernie is already in the Set
sesame.add('Ernie');           // => ['Kermit', 'Bert', 'Ernie']
sesame.intersection(muppets); // => ['Kermit']
sesame.containsAll(muppets);   // => false
```

The Queue, which is in dart:collection instead of core, is an Iterable that can be manipulated at the beginning.

```
primitives/queue.dart
var muppets = new Queue.from(['Piggy', 'Rolf']);
muppets.addFirst('Kermit');
// muppets => ['Kermit', 'Piggy', 'Rolf']

muppets.removeFirst();
muppets.removeLast();
// muppets => ['Piggy']
```

The corollary to the existence of Queue is that regular lists cannot be manipulated at the beginning. That is, there is no shift or unshift method for List. (Technically List has insert() and remove(), which take index parameters, making it possible, but ugly, to manipulate the beginning of a list.)

Dates

Dart brings some much needed sanity to dates and times in the browser. The answer to the question that is burning in many a JavaScript refugee's heart is "yes"—the first month is, in fact, 1. Let the rejoicing commence.

The niceties of Dart dates do not end there. For instance, there are a number of ways to create dates.

```
primitives/dates.dart
var mar = DateTime.parse('2013-03-01 14:31:12');
// 2013-03-01 14:31:12.000
var now = new DateTime.now();
// 2012-12-31 23:59:59.149
var apr = new DateTime(2013, 4, 1);
// 2013-04-01 00:00:00.000
var may = new DateTime(2013, 5, 1, 18, 18, 18);
// 2013-05-01 18:18:18.000
```

Even better, manipulating dates is not only possible but quite nice.

```
var jun = new DateTime(2013, 6, 1, 0, 0, 0, 0);
var jul = new DateTime(2013, 7, 1, 0, 0, 0, 0);
```

```
var diff = jul.difference(jun);
diff.inDays; // => 30

jul.add(new Duration(days: 15)); // => 2013-07-16
```

The difference() method in DateTime returns a Duration object that encapsulates a period of time. A Duration can be queried in any number of time units—from days all the way down to milliseconds. As you can see with our add() example, Durations also come in handy when adding or removing time from a particular date.

Working with dates in Dart is not a thing to dread. As you can already see, they are downright pleasant.

Types

If you had heard that Dart was a statically typed language, you might be very confused at this point. None of the code that we have written so far declares a single type. Thanks to copious use of the var keyword, our code is blissfully type-free. So what's the deal?

Dart is not, in reality, statically typed. It is sneakily typed. To understand what that means, consider the following code.

```
primitives/types.dart
var muppet = 'Piggy';

// Dart, like JavaScript, allows this, but come on!
muppet = 42;
```

We can infer that var indicates a variable type. In other words, not only are we not specifying a type, but we are telling the interpreter that the type can change. So what happens when we declare muppet to have String type?

```
String muppet = 'Piggy';
muppet = 42;
/* What happens now????! */
```

Well, it turns out that nothing happens. The String variable is now assigned a number. We can merrily perform math with that variable and all is well:

```
muppet + 17;
// 59
```

If you are coming from a statically typed language such as Java, you are likely appalled that this works. If you hail from a dynamically typed language such as JavaScript, you might feel right at home. Even the most ardent dynamic typing supporter has to admit that it is almost certainly a bug to treat a variable declared as a String as if it were a number. And Dart is quite adept at catching typing bugs like this.

The dartanalyzer tool from the SDK will point out the problem right away:

```
[warning] A value of type 'int' cannot be assigned to a variable of type 'String'
(/code/primitives/types.dart, line 34, col 16)
```

Better still, if you are using the Dart Editor, problem files are immediately flagged in the sidebar.

Problems are also flagged in the code itself.

```
String muppet = 'Piggy';
muppet = 42;
/* What happens now????! */
```

And we can mouse over the warning icon to find out exactly what the problem is.

```
String muppet = 'Piggy';
'int' is not assignable to 'String'
/* What happens now????! */
```

Dart is capable of tracing this type of information through multiple levels of function calls. Over the long term, these kinds of small wins add up a lot for keeping code robust. This is why Dart's typing is sneaky. We do not need to use it, but life is that much better if we do.

> **Tip**
>
> Important: When run normally by the SDK or the browser (for example, Dartium), type checking is *disabled*. Dart's type checking is implemented as runtime assertions. Were those checks enabled in "production" mode, performance of the application would degrade. It is still possible to catch typing errors with proper use of the Dart Editor and dartanalyzer. It is even possible to run Dartium with type checking enabled. To do so, start Dartium from the command line with DART_FLAGS='--enable_type_checks --enable_asserts' /path/to/dartium.

Although the var keyword is acceptable, it is generally considered good manners to declare types.

```
int i = 0;
bool is_done = false;
String muppet = 'Piggy';
DateTime now = new DateTime.now();
```

For types that contain other types, it is possible to declare both the container type and the containee type.

```
HashMap<String,bool> is_awesome = {
  'Scooter': false,
  'Bert': true,
  'Ernie': false
};
```

```
List<int> primes = [1,2,3,5,7,11];
```

It could be argued that too much type information makes the code harder to read—there are definitely more characters used in the above examples than a simple var. That said, the *intent* of the code is clearer.

Ultimately Dart's sneaky typing allows us to use type information as appropriate. When first prototyping applications, type information may very well be more trouble than it is worth. In small functions, type information can also get in the way. But when our applications are ready for prime time or our libraries are ready to be used by the world, type information is invaluable.

What's Next

There was a lot jammed into this chapter. Much of Dart should still feel familiar at this point, with some key but (I hope) welcome differences.

Before getting back to building our web application, let's take a quick look at functions and functional programming in Dart. At first glance, they look very much like their counterparts in JavaScript. But as you will see, there is some impressive syntactic sugar in them that is sure to increase developer joy.

CHAPTER 3

Functional Programming in Dart

Some of what makes JavaScript special is its support for functional programming. Since Dart aims to be familiar, let's examine what it is like to program functionally in Dart.

We begin with the old standby, the Fibonacci sequence. In JavaScript, this might be written like so:

```javascript
function fib(i) {
  if (i < 2) return i;
  return fib(i-2) + fib(i-1);
}
```

The Fibonacci sequence is a wonderful example for exploring the functional programming nature of a language since it, er, is a function but also because it demonstrates how to invoke a function because of its recursive nature.

I won't bother describing recursion or the particulars of this function.[1] Instead, let's focus on how to use the function in JavaScript.

```javascript
fib(1) // => 1
fib(3) // => 2
fib(10) // => 55
```

So, JavaScript functions are simple enough. They are introduced with the function keyword, followed by the name of the function, the list of supported arguments in parentheses, and the block that describes the body of the function.

So, what would the equivalent Dart version look like?

---

1. The Fibonacci sequence is well documented elsewhere if you need a refresher: http://en.wikipedia.org/wiki/Fibonacci_number.

functional_programming/fib.dart

```
// Dart
fib(i) {
  if (i < 2) return i;
  return fib(i-2) + fib(i-1);
}
```

Wait, how is that different from the JavaScript version?

```
function fib(i) {
  if (i < 2) return i;
  return fib(i-2) + fib(i-1);
}
```

Astute readers will note that the Dart version lacks the function keyword. Aside from that, the two function definitions are identical, as is invoking the two.

```
fib(1); // => 1
```

```
fib(5); // => 5
```

```
fib(10); // => 55
```

If nothing else, we can see that the designers of the Dart language have certainly succeeded in producing something familiar.

Anonymous Functions

The experienced JavaScript programmer is well versed in using anonymous functions. Since functions in JavaScript are a first-order concept, functions are passed around in JavaScript with abandon. Some even lament the callback hell of certain frameworks, but aesthetics aside, there can be no denying that anonymous functions are an important thing in JavaScript. So, the same must surely be true in Dart, right?

In JavaScript, an anonymous function omits the function name, using only the function keyword.

```
function(i) {
  if (i < 2) return i;
  return fib(i-2) + fib(i-1);
}
```

We have already seen that the only difference between JavaScript and Dart functions is that the latter do not have the function keyword. It turns out this is also the only difference between JavaScript and Dart anonymous functions.

functional_programming/fib.dart

```
(i) {
  if (i < 2) return i;
```

```
  return fib(i-2) + fib(i-1);
}
```

At first glance, that looks quite odd—almost naked. But that is just our JavaScript eye. Ruby has lambdas and procs that look very similar.

```
{ |i| $stderr.puts i }
```

Given enough consideration, what purpose does the function keyword in Java-Script really serve? The knee-jerk reaction is that it helps to identify the anonymous function, but in practice, it is just noise.

Consider this Fibonacci printer:

```
var list = [1, 5, 8, 10];
list.forEach(function(i) {fib_printer(i)});

function fib_printer(i) {
  console.log("Fib(" + i + "): " + fib(i));
}

function fib(i) {
  if (i < 2) return i;
  return fib(i-2) + fib(i-1);
}
```

Does the function keyword help or hinder readability of the code? Clearly, it makes the situation worse, especially inside the forEach() call.

Let's consider the equivalent Dart code.

```
var list = [1, 5, 8, 10];
list.forEach((i) {fib_printer(i);});

fib_printer(i) {
  print("Fib($i): ${fib(i)}");
}

fib(i) {
  if (i < 2) return i;
  return fib(i-2) + fib(i-1);
}
```

> **Tip**
>
> Note: We are using the string interpolation trick first noted in Chapter 1, *Project: Your First Dart Application*, on page 3 to insert the value of the counter i into "Fib($i)".

All that we did was remove the function keyword, and yet the intent of the code is much clearer. Multiply that effect across an entire project, and the long-term health of a codebase goes up dramatically.

Speaking of clarity, if curly braces make you cringe, there is a hash rocket syntax that can be used for *simple* functions. Instead of writing our anonymous iterator as (i) { fib_printer(i) }, we can write (i) => fib_printer(i). Thus, our code becomes as follows:

```
var list = [1, 5, 8, 10];
list.forEach((i) => fib_printer(i));

fib_printer(i) {
  print("Fib($i): ${fib(i)}");
}

fib(i) {
  if (i < 2) return i;
  return fib(i-2) + fib(i-1);
}
```

The argument (i) is repeated both in the definition of the anonymous function and in the call to fib_printer(i). In JavaScript, there is nothing to be done to clean that up. In Dart, however, the function (i) => fib_printer(i) can be further simplified as simply fib_printer.

```
var list = [1, 5, 8, 10];
list.forEach(fib_printer);

fib_printer(i) {
  print("Fib($i): ${fib(i)}");
}

fib(i) {
  if (i < 2) return i;
  return fib(i-2) + fib(i-1);
}
```

That is a fantastic little shortcut to use with abandon in our Dart code.

First-Order Functions

Passing an anonymous function into an iterator like forEach() already demonstrates some nice support for first-class objects—the ability to treat functions as variables that can be assigned and passed around.

Dart's functional programming capabilities are strong enough to support things like partial function application. The classic example of partial application is converting an add() function that returns the sum of three numbers into another function that fixes one of those numbers.

functional_programming/first_order.dart

```
add(x, y, z) {
  return x + y + z;
}
makeAdder2(fn, arg1) {
  return (y, z) {
    return fn(arg1, y, z);
  };
}
var add10 = makeAdder2(add, 10);
```

The name *partial application* comes from returning a function with one argument already applied. In this case, the makeAdder2 function returns another function taking two arguments. The result of calling this new function is the same as calling the original function with the first argument fixed to arg1.

At this point, the add10() function takes two numbers, sums them, and ups the total by 10.

```
add10(1,1); // => 12
```

In addition to partial application, it is also possible, though still a little awkward, to use other functional programming techniques like combinators and dynamic currying. For the interested, an example of this would be the curry package: http://pub.dartlang.org/packages/curry.

Optional Arguments

One of the more tedious chores in most languages is extracting optional arguments. Dart's take on the matter is an altogether pleasant built-in syntax.

Let's say that we want a function named good_day() to print a pleasant greeting, with an optional flag to indicate a follow-up message. Calling such a function in Dart looks like the following.

functional_programming/optional.dart

```
good_day("Bob");
// Good day, Bob.
good_day("Bob", emphatic: true);
// Good day, Bob.
// I said good day!
```

In the second call, we supply the optional emphatic: true option to get the extra message. At first glance, this might look like a HashMap. Closer inspection reveals that there are no curly braces around it. This is not a HashMap, though the similarity is intentional. Rather this is Dart's built-in syntax to supply an optional parameter.

To declare a parameter as optional in a function definition, wrap it inside curly braces. The good_day() function, with a required name parameter and an optional emphatic parameter, can be defined as:

```
good_day(name, {emphatic}) {
  print("Good day, ${name}.");
  if (emphatic) {
    print("I said good day!");
  }
}
```

This is a wonderful syntax. At the same time, it is easy to understand what is intended and there is very little clutter. Even if you are new to Dart, the curly braces evoke a sense of named parameters by virtue of their resemblance to JSON object literals. With this, the body of the function can focus on its inherent purpose—no options parsing to obscure intent.

Named optional parameters support more than one value by separating them with commas. It is even possible to supply default values by including a colon after the parameter name.

Consider the following profile(), which prints out a name and, optionally, a personal hero and favorite color. Since Weird Al Yankovic is the personal hero to a majority of hipsters, we can supply him as the default value as follows:

```
profile(name, {hero:"Weird Al", favorite_color}) {
  print("Name: ${name}");
  print("  personal hero: ${hero}");
  if (favorite_color != null) {
    print("  favorite color: ${favorite_color}");
  }
}
```

With that, if we profile Bob, we find:

```
profile("Bob");
// Name: Bob
//   personal hero: Weird Al
```

Should Bob prove fickle and change his personal hero and decide upon a favorite color, a subsequent call to profile() might result in:

```
profile("Bob", favorite_color: 'Purple', hero: 'Frank Drebin');
// Name: Bob
//   personal hero: Frank Drebin
//   favorite color: Purple
```

Named, optional parameters are an exceptional aid for writing clean code, but Dart does not stop there. Dart also supports positional parameters. That is, if we want the first parameter to a function to be required but the next two to be optional, then Dart has us covered.

Since named, optional parameters adopt a HashMap feel, it should not be a surprise that positional, optional parameters adopt a List feel. So, instead of curly braces, we use square brackets in the function definition:

```
movie(title, [starring="Leslie Nielson", co_starring]) {
  print("Great movie: ${title}");
  print("  Starring: ${starring}");
  if (co_starring != null) {
    print("  Co-starring: ${co_starring}");
  }
}
```

As you can see, positional parameters also support default values—though an equals sign is used instead of a colon. Calling this function is a simple matter of invoking it with just the required value or one or more of the optional values.

```
movie("The Naked Gun");
// Great movie: The Naked Gun
//    Starring: Leslie Nielson
movie("Airplane!", "Robert Hays", "Leslie Nielson");
// Great movie: The Naked Gun
//    Starring: Robert Hays
//    Co-starring: Leslie Nielson
```

This certainly beats rooting through object literals. Optional arguments are even more powerful inside class and instance methods, as you'll see in Chapter 7, *Classes and Objects*, on page 59.

| Tip | Note: this make sense in Dart. One of the ways in which Dart departs from JavaScript is in the use of the this keyword. Dart's stance on the matter is that this has absolutely nothing to do with the current function. Instead, this is reserved for objects and always refers to the current object. There is no binding of this, applying this, or calling this in Dart. In other words, this has nothing to do with functions. We'll discuss this again in *Classes and Objects*, but only briefly because this is so dang simple in Dart! |

What's Next

In many ways, this chapter is a work very much in progress. Dart lacks quite a lot of the power that is currently available to the JavaScript programmer: there is no reflection, and there is no arguments property available inside functions.

You can already see that, even lacking these, Dart is extremely powerful in what it does allow you to do. We'll return to this topic again in Chapter 11, *Project: Varying Behavior*, on page 103.

CHAPTER 4

Manipulating the DOM

We can't write web applications without accessing and manipulating the DOM.[1] Sadly, Dart can't do away entirely with established and often maddening aspects of the DOM API. Happily, Dart does provide a compatibility library that reestablishes some sanity when manipulating web pages.

dart:html

The library that we will use to interact and manipulate objects in a web page is dart:html. We will talk more about libraries in Chapter 10, *Libraries*, on page 93. For now, just think of them like libraries from any other language (except JavaScript, of course)—a mechanism for encapsulating logically and physically separate functionality.

The dart:html library is not your grandmother's DOM API. The dart:html core library is Dart's take on what DOM programming should have been like from the beginning.

Finding Things

The primary entry points into DOM are document.query() and document.queryAll(). Both take a CSS selector as the argument. The former returns a single matching element; the latter returns a list of all matching elements. Here are some simple examples:

```
dom/finding.dart
document.query('h1');              // => First <h1> in the document
document.query('#people-list');    // => Element with id of 'people-list'
document.query('.active');         // => First element with 'active' class
document.queryAll('h2');           // => All <h2> elements
```

---

1. Document Object Model: http://en.wikipedia.org/wiki/Document_Object_Model

The query() and queryAll() methods are actually methods of the Element class. Document, like every other class representing a bit of the DOM, subclasses Element. In practice, this means we can limit queries to a specific element by first finding the element and then querying from it.

```
var list = document.query('ul#people-list');
var last_person = list.query(':last-child');
last_person.innerHtml;
// => 'Lucy'
```

Or we can chain it:

```
document.
  query('ul#people-list').
  query(':last-child').
  innerHtml;
// => 'Lucy'
```

This Is Not jQuery

Chaining query() methods like this might suggest a jQuery-like composability, but these are not wrapped sets. Consider trying to highlight the name of people in an unordered list. In jQuery, we might write something like this:

```
$('li', 'ul#people-list).
  attr('class', 'highlight');
```

In Dart, we have to manually iterate over each element:

```
document.
  query('ul#people-list').
  queryAll('li').
  forEach((li) {
    li.classes.add('highlight');
  });
```

Although Dart makes working with the DOM easier than working with pure JavaScript, there are still some things that jQuery does a little better.

The bottom line with finding elements on a page in Dart is that query() and queryAll() do pretty much what you expect, making it easy to query the DOM.

Adding Things

Although Dart supports the usual Element and Node classes for manipulating the DOM, Dart goes out of its way to allow us to stick to just an Element class. For just about any HTML element, Dart defines a convenience constructor. To create a <div>, for instance, there is the DivElement constructor. Coupled with text and innerHtml properties, it's easy to get started with DOM elements.

```
dom/adding.dart
var gallery = new DivElement();
gallery.text = 'Welcome to the Gallery';
```

For a more general purpose way to create a new element in Dart, we can use the handy html named constructor for Element.

```
var gallery = new Element.html('<div id="gallery">');
```

The Element.html() named constructor does not restrict us to creating a single element. We can create more complex HTML to be inserted into the page.

```
var gallery = new Element.html("""
  <div id="gallery">
    <ul>
      <li><img src="img01.png">
      <li><img src="img02.png">
      <li><img src="img03.png">
      <!-- ... -->
    </ul>
  </div>""");
```

Dart's string interpolation is especially handy when building larger HTML fragments. The result can be almost template-like.

```
gallery(title, photographer) {
  return new Element.html("""
    <div id="gallery">
      <h2>${title}</h2>
      <ul>
        <li><img src="img01.png"/>
        <li><img src="img02.png"/>
        <li><img src="img03.png"/>
        <!-- ... -->
      </ul>
      <h3 class="footer">
        Photos by: ${photographer}
      </h3>
    </div>""");
}
```

To insert an element into the document, use the append() method exposed by Element.

```
var gallery = new Element.html('<div id="gallery">');
document.
  query('#content').
  append(gallery);
```

When more sophisticated element insertion is needed, Dart supports the standard insertAdjacentHTML() method.[2] This is far more verbose than the jQuery prepend(), append(), before(), and after() Element methods. Even the somewhat shorter insertAdjacentElement() suffers by comparison to the jQuery equivalent.

```
var gallery = new Element.html('<div id="gallery">');
document.
  query('#content').
  insertAdjacentElement('afterBegin', gallery);
```

The previous code would insert the gallery element at the beginning of the content <div>'s nodes (equivalent to jQuery's prepend()).

Creating elements in Dart is quite nice. Appending them to the document or a list of elements is also pretty easy. Dart still leaves something to be desired when we need to perform more sophisticated insertion of elements. Hopefully, this will improve as Dart evolves.

Removing Things

Removing an element from the document is quite Darty.

```
dom/removing.dart
document.
  query('#content').
  query('#gallery').
  remove();
```

This would find the element with the ID of "content"; then, inside that, it would find the "gallery" element and remove it from the page. If the page began:

```
<body>
<div id="content">
  <div id="gallery"/>
  <p class="instructions">...</p>
</div>
</body>
```

then the result of the previous remove() would be as follows:

```
<body>
<div id="content">
  <p class="instructions">...</p>
</div>
</body>
```

Not being required to walk up to an element's parent to remove the element, as we have to do in JavaScript, is a nice win.

---

2.   https://developer.mozilla.org/en/DOM/Element.insertAdjacentHTML

Updating Elements

We have already discussed adding and removing elements from a parent element. Aside from those actions, the most common manipulation is adding and removing CSS classes on an element. The following would remove the subdued class from the <blockquote> tag and add the highlighted class to it:

```
dom/updating.dart
document.
  query('blockquote').
  classes.
  remove('subdued');

document.
  query('blockquote').
  classes.
  add('highlighted');
```

Here, we again see the difference between Dart's set-based approach to classes and jQuery's chainable approach. In jQuery, removing and adding classes could be accomplished in a single statement with several chains. In Dart (for now) we are forced to use two separate statements. Actually, that is not 100 percent true, but we'll come back to that in a bit.

In addition to manipulating classes, the Element class allows for the familiar innerHTML change—except that in Dart, it is innerHtml.

```
document.
  query('blockquote').
  innerHtml = 'Four score and <u>seven</u> years ago...';
```

The reason that it is innerHtml in Dart is that all methods are camel-cased in Dart. Rather than sticking slavishly to obscure names, Dart makes life easier for us by opting for a sane convention.

Manipulating classes and updating innerHtml covers the most common cases of changing an element directly. If more is needed, then the Element class[3] is the place to start looking.

Method Cascades

In the previous section, you found that Dart's lack of built-in jQuery-like wrapped sets forces you to add and remove classes in two separate steps. Although Dart's Element class does not support wrapped sets, Dart's object system does support something very similar—method cascades.

---

3.   http://api.dartlang.org/html/Element.html

Method cascades let us call several methods on the same objects. A method cascade is invoked with two dots (..) instead of the one dot that calls a method. Here's the cascaded version of the code that added and removed classes.

```
document.
  query('blockquote').
  classes
    ..remove('subdued')
    ..add('highlighted');
```

That is much more compact and, surprisingly, more readable. It is obvious at a glance that we are performing two operations on the classes property. Best of all, we can use cascades on *any* Dart object—not just Element operations.

Methods cascades are very powerful—you will definitely see them again.

DOM Ready

There is no need for an on-DOM-ready handler in Dart. Dart makes the sane decision of deferring evaluation until the DOM is ready for processing.

Actually, Dart takes this a step further. Dart allows one <script> tag of type application/dart with one main() entry point. This one entry point is what is invoked when the DOM is ready.

Folks coming from the craziness of JavaScript with an infinite number of <script> tags and execution contexts may be feeling a desperate sense of constriction at this point. But after a deep breath or two, cooler heads should be able to admit that an infinite number of scripts all running at essentially the same time usually wind up causing more trouble than they are worth. Besides, Dart does allow for multiple, *isolated* execution environments, as you'll see in Chapter 14, *Futures and Isolates*, on page 127.

Be wary of compiling Dart to JavaScript and then expecting <script> tags that point to this compiled JavaScript to work. We will talk about how Dart's JavaScript compiler maintains this single, main entry point in the next chapter, *Dart and JavaScript*.

What's Next

The Dart HTML library exposes a familiar yet powerfully different means for manipulating web pages. It is not a complete, high-level solution like jQuery, but it provides a much nicer foundation on which to build higher-level libraries. In the next chapter, let's build on what we have so far and see how Dart supports the modern Web by compiling Dart into cross-browser Java-Script *applications*.

CHAPTER 5

Dart and JavaScript

When Dart first came out, every major browser vendor, as well as the WebKit project, announced that they had absolutely no intention of embedding the Dart VM in their browsers. Many bristled at the very suggestion that a non-standard language[1] be supported even obliquely. How another language was supposed to become a standard seemed a tricky question. Fortunately, Google had a plan.

In the grand tradition of CoffeeScript,[2] the Dart project includes a compiler capable of compiling Dart into JavaScript. The goal is that, even if Dart does not become an overnight standard, web developers tired of the quirks of JavaScript have a choice. We can now code in a modern language for the Web but still support the wide variety of browsers on the market.

The JavaScript generated by the Dart compiler includes shim code for the various Dart libraries. There is generated JavaScript that translates Dart DOM calls into JavaScript. There is generated JavaScript that supports Dart Ajax. For just about every feature of Dart, there is a corresponding chunk of JavaScript that gets included in the compiled output.

If that sounds large, well, it is. When first released, the compiler generated tens of thousands of lines of JavaScript!

Of course, the compiler continues to improve. It now supports compression/optimization and is producing JavaScript libraries in the range of thousands of lines of code instead of tens of thousands. Considering that Dart does a good chunk of the work of many JavaScript libraries like jQuery, this is already a good start. And it is only going to get better.

---

1. Dart is now a standard supported by the same ECMA organization that is responsible for the JavaScript standard: http://www.ecma-international.org/publications/standards/Ecma-408.htm.
2. http://coffeescript.org/

Compiling to JavaScript with dart2js

The tool provided to compile Dart down into JavaScript is dart2js. The dart2js compiler can be found among the Dart software development kit builds.[3] The SDK are the ones with "sdk" in the filename (as opposed to the "editor" builds that include the editor in addition to the SDK).

We see that, once unzipped, the SDK contains the entire Dart library (core, html, io, json).

```
+-- bin
    +-- dart
    +-- dart2js
    +-- dartanalyzer
    +-- dartdoc
    +-- pub
+-- include
+-- lib
|   +-- async
|   +-- chrome
|   +-- collection
|   +-- convert
|   +-- core
|   +-- html
|   +-- indexed_db
|   +-- io
|   +-- isolate
|   +-- js
|   +-- json
|   +-- math
|   +-- mirrors
|   +-- svg
|   +-- typed_data
|   +-- utf
|   +-- web_audio
|   +-- web_gl
|   +-- web_sql
+-- util
```

In addition to the core Dart libraries, the SDK contains library code to support documentation (dartdoc) and compiling to JavaScript (dart2js).

Using dart2js could not be more basic. It takes a single command-line argument—the Dart filename. There is also a single command-line option that can be used to set the filename of the resulting JavaScript (out.js by default):

```
$ dart2js -omain.dart.js main.dart
```

---

3. https://www.dartlang.org/tools/sdk/

There is no output from the compiler indicating success, but we now have a nice little JavaScript version of our script.

```
$ ls -lh
-rw-r--r-- 1 chris chris   33 Feb 17 12:47 main.dart
-rw-r--r-- 1 chris chris 7.2K Feb 17 12:47 main.dart.js
```

Well, maybe it's not "little."

If there are errors in the Dart code being compiled, dart2js does a very nice job of letting us know where the errors occur.

```
$ dart2js main.dart
main.dart:5:3: Warning: Cannot resolve "document".
  document.query('#foo');
  ^^^^^^^^
```

One thing to bear in mind when compiling JavaScript is that dart2js works only at the application level, not the class level. Consider the situation in which we are converting our comic book collection application to follow a hip MVC pattern.

```
comics.dart
Collection.Comics.dart
HipsterModel.dart
Models.ComicBook.dart
Views.AddComic.dart
Views.AddComicForm.dart
Views.ComicsCollection.dart
```

There is no way to compile individual classes into usable JavaScript.

```
$ dart2js Models.ComicBook.dart
Models.ComicBook.dart:1:1: Error: Could not find "main".
library models_comic_book;

Error: Compilation failed.
```

If the script containing the main() entry point references the other libraries or if those libraries reference other libraries, then everything will be slurped into the resulting JavaScript. The three libraries referenced in the following import statements will be pulled into the compiled JavaScript:

javascript/web/scripts/comics.dart
```
import 'Collections.Comics.dart' as Collections;
import 'Views.Comics.dart' as Views;

main() {
  // ...

}
```

Similarly, the ComicBook model will also be included in the dart2js-generated JavaScript by virtue of being referenced in the collection class.

javascript/web/scripts/Collections.Comics.dart

```
library comics_collection;

import 'HipsterCollection.dart';
import 'Models.ComicBook.dart';

class Comics extends HipsterCollection {
  // ...

}
```

At some point, it might be nice to write classes in Dart and compile them into usable JavaScript. For now, however, we are relegated to compiling entire applications, not pieces.

Maintaining Dart and JavaScript Side by Side

As Dart and dart2js evolve, the performance of the generated JavaScript will improve. At this early stage, Dart code compiled to JavaScript rivals and sometimes surpasses code a typical JavaScripter might write.[4] But as fast as the compiled JavaScript gets, it will never be as fast as running Dart natively.

The question then becomes, how can we send Dart code to Dart-enabled browsers and send the compiled JavaScript to other browsers?

The answer is relatively simple: include a small JavaScript snippet that detects the absence of Dart and loads the corresponding JavaScript. As you saw in the previous section, if we compile a main.dart script, then dart2js will produce a corresponding main.dart.js JavaScript version.

The following JavaScript snippet will do the trick (placed after the closing </body> tag):

```
if (!/Dart/.test(navigator.userAgent)) {
  loadJsEquivalentScripts();
}

function loadJsEquivalentScripts() {
  var scripts = document.getElementsByTagName('script');
  for (var i=0; i<scripts.length; i++) {
    loadJsEquivalent(scripts[i]);
  }
}
```

---

4. See the Dart performance page for details on how that is determined: https://www.dart-lang.org/performance/.

```
function loadJsEquivalent(script) {
  if (!script.hasAttribute('src')) return;
  if (!script.hasAttribute('type')) return;
  if (script.getAttribute('type') != 'application/dart') return;

  var js_script = document.createElement('script');
  js_script.setAttribute('src', script.getAttribute('src') + '.js');
  document.body.appendChild(js_script);
}
```

There is a similar script in Dart core.[5] In most cases, that script should be preferred over ours because it does other things (such as start the Dart engine).

The check for an available Dart engine is a simple matter of checking the user agent string. If it contains the word "Dart," then it is Dart-enabled.

```
if (!/Dart/.test(navigator.userAgent))
```

That may come in handy elsewhere in our Dart adventures.

The remainder of the JavaScript is fairly simple. The loadJsEquivalentScripts() function invokes loadJsEquivalent() for every <script> tag in the DOM. This method has a few guard clauses to ensure that a Dart script is in play. It then appends a new .js <script> to the DOM to trigger the equivalent JavaScript load.

To use that JavaScript detection script, we save it as dart.js and add it to the web page containing the Dart <script> tag.

```
<script src="/scripts/dart.js"></script>
```

```
<script src="/scripts/main.dart"
        type="application/dart"></script>
```

A Dart-enabled browser will evaluate and execute main.dart directly. Other browsers will ignore the unknown "application/dart" type and instead execute the code in dart.js, creating new <script> tags that source the main.dart.js file that we compiled with dart2js.

In the end, we have superfast code for browsers that support Dart. For both Dart and non-Dart browsers, we have elegant, structured, modern code. Even this early in Dart's evolution, we get the best of both worlds.

---

5. It is part of the browser Pub package available at: http://pub.dartlang.org/packages/browser. We will talk more about Pub and library packages in Chapter 10, *Libraries*, on page 93.

Using JavaScript in Dart

Programmers new to Dart often look for a jQuery-like library or a way to call jQuery directly from Dart. As you have already seen, Dart's built-in DOM support obviates the need for jQuery, but there are still times when it is useful to call JavaScript from Dart. Happily, Dart makes this easy with the dart:js package.

We will talk more about libraries and packages in Chapter 10, *Libraries*, on page 93. For now it is enough to know that we need to import the dart:js package to interact with JavaScript:

javascript/test/calling_javascript_test.dart
```
import 'dart:js';
```

Since JavaScript throws everything into a top-level namespace, dart:js makes this available through its context property. This property provides access to top-level JavaScript variables, classes, and functions.

Let's first try to call a JavaScript function from Dart. Consider a simple add() function that adds two numbers in JavaScript:

javascript/lib/add.js
```
function add(num1, num2) {
  return num1 + num2;
}
```

Calling this from Dart is a simple matter of importing dart:js and using the callMethod() method on the top-level JavaScript context object. In the case of the add() method, we want to call it by name, supplying it with two arguments:

javascript/test/calling_javascript_test.dart
```
import 'dart:js';

// ...

var answer = context.callMethod('add', [19, 23]);
```

After executing this line, answer will be the integer 42. What is especially nice here is that the JavaScript compatibility library takes care of assigning the proper type to the value back in Dart.

The top-level JavaScript context variable is a JavaScript proxy object. It should come as no surprise that Dart facilitates creating our own JavaScript object proxies. Consider a simple Person in JavaScript:

```
javascript/lib/person.js
function Person(name) {
  this.name = name;
  this.greet = function() {
    return 'Howdy, ' + this.name + '!';
  };
}
```

We can instantiate—with constructor arguments—a JavaScript proxy in Dart with dart:js's JsObject wrapper:

```
var person = new JsObject(context['Person'], ['Bob']);
```

To invoke the JavaScript greet() method, we again use callMethod(), this time on the Person wrapper instead of context:

```
person.callMethod('greet', []);
// => 'Howdy, Bob!'
```

Setting properties on JavaScript objects is even easier. We simply use the square bracket operator to look up and assign JavaScript properties:

```
person['name'] = 'Fred';

person.callMethod('greet', []);
// => 'Howdy, Fred!'
```

Lest we Dart programmers forget, JavaScript is the land of callback hell. So, from time to time it will be necessary for a JavaScript function or method to invoke a callback function. In most cases, dart:js lets us supply a *Dart* function to serve as a callback.

Examining the following simple JavaScript multiply(), we see that it takes two arguments, a numeric multiplier and a callback function:

```
javascript/lib/add.js
function multiply(multiplier, cb) {
  return multiplier * cb();
}
```

The result of this function is the multiplication product of multiplier and the result of the callback function cb().

Given a very simple Dart function that computes 84 divided by 4, we can call the callback-laden multiply() function from Dart as:

```
var answer = context.callMethod('multiply', [2, ()=> 84/4]);
```

Yet again, the answer in Dart will be 42.

Dart's JavaScript compatibility library is surprisingly easy. There are some limitations, however, mostly the kinds of values that can be sent back and forth. But even these limitations are not as restrictive as might be expected. Basic types (numbers, Booleans, and strings) can be sent to and from Java-Script. It is also possible to send DOM elements and collections, which comes in extremely handy when working with JavaScript browser libraries. It is even possible to send events, blobs, image data, and more!

More often than not, Dart and JavaScript interoperability just works as expected. Even though we might prefer writing Dart, we do not want to rewrite the wheel if someone else has already done it for us in JavaScript.

What's Next

The ability to compile Dart into JavaScript means that we do not have to wait for a tipping point of browser support before enjoying the power of Dart. Today, we can start writing web applications in Dart and expect that they will work for everyone. Plus, we can leverage existing codebases in JavaScript with ease. JavaScript compatibility is a good thing because, in the next chapters, we will be taking our simple Dart application to the next level and we wouldn't want to leave our nonhipster friends too far behind.

Part II

Effective Coding Techniques

With the basics of Dart out of the way, we'll explore what makes Dart unique. We'll begin by converting the simple application from Chapter 1 into a full-blown MVC client library. Happily, this is quite easy to do in Dart.

With the MVC library started, it's high time we discuss some of Dart's most exciting features: the excellent object-oriented programming support and a customizable events system.

CHAPTER 6

Project: MVC in Dart

In this chapter, you'll get your first real feel for what it means to write Dart code. Until now, our discussion has not strayed far from the familiar—or at least from what is similar to JavaScript.

We'll take the very simple comic book collection application from Chapter 1, *Project: Your First Dart Application*, on page 3 and convert it to an MVC design pattern. Since this will be client based, it won't be Model-View-Controller. Rather, it will be Model-Collection-View, plus a Router, similar to Backbone.js.

We'll start by implementing collections of objects in Dart and then describe the objects themselves. Once we have the foundation in place, we'll take a look at views and templates.

This is another "project" chapter, so we'll gloss over some Dart details to focus on writing code.

MVC in Dart

The foundation of our Hipster MVC library (of course that's the name) will be collections of objects, not the objects themselves. The collection maps nicely onto REST-like web services, resulting in a clean API for adding, deleting, and updating records.

Hearkening back to the first chapter, our comics collection can be retrieved via an HTTP GET of /comics. In Hipster MVC parlance, we will call that a fetch().

With REST-like resources, we can also refer to /comics as the URL root because it serves as the root for all operations on the collection of individual records. This is shown in the following sketches.

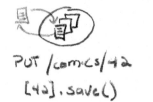

Adding a new comic to the collection is an HTTP POST operation on /comics. And, in hipster-ese, that is an add().

To update a comic book with new information, we use HTTP's PUT, supplying the ID in the subpath of the URL: PUT /comics/42. From Hipster MVC's perspective, we retrieve the record, update it, and save it with save().

Lastly, to remove a record from the collection, we use the destroy() method. This will result in an HTTP DELETE. Again we use the collection URL including the ID.

Let's get started writing that code.

Hipster Collections

Recall from *Project: Your First Dart Application* that our comics.dart looks something like this:

```
your_first_dart_app/web/scripts/skel.dart
import 'dart:html';
import 'dart:convert';
main() {
  // Do stuff here
}
```

We replaced the // Do stuff here comment with code that retrieves the comic book collection from /comics and displays it on the web page. In MVC, the collection object retrieves the records, and a view object displays the contents of the collection.

```
mvc/web/scripts/comics.dart
import 'dart:html';
import 'dart:convert';
import 'dart:collection';
main() {
  var comics_view, comics_collection;
```

```
comics_collection = new ComicsCollection(
  onChange: ()=> comics_view.render()
);
comics_view = new ComicsView(
  el: document.query('#comics-list'),
  collection: comics_collection
);
comics_collection.fetch();

}
```

This is a first pass at MVC, not a final product. Already, it is quite promising. The ComicsCollection class needs very little construction—just a callback that re-renders the collection view when the collection changes. Similarly, ComicsView needs only an element on the page to which it can attach itself and, of course, a reference to the collection that it will display.

With both the collection and view constructed, we fetch the collection from the REST-like back-end server. Once the response comes back, the collection will be populated, resulting in a change. This change will invoke our callback, which will update the view. That is fairly tidy, which is the benefit of using an MVC pattern, after all.

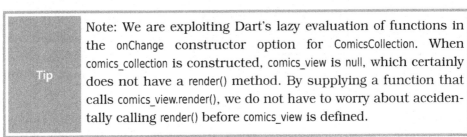

Tip

Note: We are exploiting Dart's lazy evaluation of functions in the onChange constructor option for ComicsCollection. When comics_collection is constructed, comics_view is null, which certainly does not have a render() method. By supplying a function that calls comics_view.render(), we do not have to worry about accidentally calling render() before comics_view is defined.

Observant readers may have noticed that we have a new import: dart:collection. As the name suggests, this library adds lots of nifty collection-related code. Since we are writing an MVC collection, that will come in quite handy, starting with the class definition:

```
class ComicsCollection extends IterableBase {

List models = [];
Iterator get iterator => models.iterator;

  // ...
}
```

> **Tip**
>
> Note: When writing scripts or initial implementations of libraries, we can easily forgo typing information. When writing libraries that we hope others will use, it is a must. To be clear, it is possible to write reusable code without the type information, but it is tantamount to being a bad Dart citizen.

Extending IterableBase and defining iterator are a cheap way to get collection-like behavior in a class. We will discuss Dart's object-oriented approach in Chapter 7, *Classes and Objects*, on page 59, but the intent of this class is already fairly self-evident. Our ComicsCollection is going to extend another class that knows different ways to iterate over a collection of things. In this case, IterableBase can iterate with methods like forEach(), map(), reduce(), and many others. All that IterableBase needs is an iterator, which our list of models provides via the List class.

"Getter" methods like iterator are methods that are invoked without the trailing parentheses. Instead of invoking it as collection.iterator(), it would be simply collection.iterator. Getters, and their counterpart setters, can be quite useful as you'll see later.

Our ComicsCollection knows how to collect model objects, but we are still missing two requirements for an MVC collection. The first is the ability to communicate when changes occur (the views need a way to know when to update). Also, this would not be a REST-like collection without some create, read, update, and delete (CRUD) methods.

At this stage in our MVC solution, our collection will communicate change via a simple callback method. Have no fear, we will lose the callbacks in Chapter 8, *Events and Streams*, on page 77. But, for now, our class's constructor will accept a callback function, assigning it to the local onChange variable:

```
class ComicsCollection extends IterableBase {
  // ...

var onChange = (){};

// Constructor method
ComicsCollection({this.onChange});

  // ...
}
```

Here, we already see a glimpse of the extraordinary power of Dart constructors in the ComicsCollection() constructor methods. First, constructors are easy—they are a method with the same name as the class. Second, they do not require a method body. Lastly, they take the optional arguments from Chapter 3, *Functional Programming in Dart*, on page 21 a step further—prefixed with this, optional arguments are assigned directly to object instance variables.

In other words, instantiating the object as new ComicsCollection(onChange: (){ print('Awesome sauce here!) }); will print "Awesome sauce here!" to the console whenever changes are made to the collection. That is an amazing lines-of-code savings over not only JavaScript, but also over most established languages. It gets even better, but we'll leave that for *Classes and Objects*. For now, let's get back to building our ComicsCollection.

Now that we have our collection behaving like a collection and capable of communicating change, let's make it behave like an Ajax-backed object. For discussion purposes, we will not go into complete CRUD but will focus on fetching the objects from the back-end data store, creating new objects in the data store and deleting them.

We already know from *Project: Your First Dart Application* how to fetch data over Ajax in Dart. In this case, when the data has loaded, we call the private _handleOnLoad() method.

```
void fetch() {
  var req = new HttpRequest();
  req.onLoad.listen((event) {
    var list = JSON.decode(req.responseText);
    _handleOnLoad(list);
  });
  req.open('get', url);
  req.send();
}
```

Instead of populating a UI element as we did in our first application, we need to behave in a more frameworky fashion. That is, we build the internal collection and notify interested parties when changes to the collection occur.

```
_handleOnLoad(list) {
  list.forEach((attrs) {
    var new_model = new ComicBook(attrs, collection: this);
    models.add(new_model);
    onChange();
  });
}
```

For each set of model attributes, we create a new model object, set the model's collection property to our current collection, and add the model to the collection's models list. Once that's complete, we invoke the onChange() callback method, telling interested parties that a change has occurred.

The model does not strictly need to know about the collection (in fact, it should not communicate directly with the collection). We assign it here so that the model can reuse the collection's URL for finding, creating, and updating back-end objects. The model will communicate with the collection via callbacks just as we have done with onChange() here.

We still need the ability to create new comic books in our collection. Most of the heavy lifting will be done by the ComicBook model. In the collection we create a new model and tell it to save itself. Upon successful save, we add it to the internal list of comic books and notify interested parties via onChange().

```
class ComicsCollection extends IterableBase {
  // ...
  create(attrs) {
    var new_model = new ComicBook(attrs, collection: this);
    new_model.save((event) {
      models.add(new_model);
      onChange();
    });
  }
  // ...
}
```

Of course, we have not even introduced the model base class yet, so let's get that out of the way next.

Hipster Models

Where the collection had a models property to store its data, the model will have the attributes property. Recall that the collection will pass the model a reference to itself, giving the model quick access to the collection's properties (for example, url). Thus, we can begin defining the model class as follows:

```
class ComicBook {
  Map attributes;
  ComicsCollection collection;

  ComicBook(this.attributes, {this.collection});
}
```

The declaration of the attributes and collection properties in this class should be familiar now. Each results in a setter/getter for ComicBook instances (for example, comic_book.collection = my_comics and comic_book.attributes['title']).

We previously saw Dart's class constructor in ComicsCollection. The constructor definition for ComicBook is very similar. There is no need for a constructor body—we assign instance variables directly in the declaration thanks to the this prefix on the variables. In this constructor declaration, the attributes are required and the collection is optional.

Since the model is Map-like, we use the [] operator to retrieve attribute values.

```
class ComicBook {
  Map attributes;
  ComicsCollection collection;

  ComicBook(this.attributes, {this.collection});

  operator [](attr) => attributes[attr];

}
```

We will talk more about operators in *Classes and Objects*, but the intent of that method is crystal clear. When we look up an attribute directly on the model (for example, comic_book['title']), the value in the attributes HashMap is returned. The hash-rocket shortcut for function bodies is extremely handy at times.

The URL for ComicBook is complicated only by the question of whether the model has an ID attribute. If it does have an ID, then we assume that the model has been previously saved in the back end. In this case, updates will be PUT against the resource root plus an ID (for example, /comics/42). Otherwise, this is a new model that will need to be POSTed to the resource root (for example, /comics). Recall also that if the model has a collection, then the URL root can come from the collection.

```
get id => attributes['id'];
String get url => isSaved ?
  "$urlRoot/$id" : urlRoot;

String get urlRoot => (collection == null) ?
  "" : collection.url;

bool get isSaved => id != null;
```

With that, we can now define the save() method. Saving a client-side model involves the following:

- An HttpRequest object, over which the model data will be sent to the back-end datastore

- JSON functions to encode the data before transport and to decode the response

- A listener for the HttpRequest object's onLoad (in other words, on success) event

- Replacing the model's attributes property with data returned from the server

- Invoking an optional callback so that the object that called save() can respond appropriately

Whoa! There is a lot going on with a simple save, and the code reflects it.

```
save([callback]) {
  var req = new HttpRequest(),
      method = isSaved ? 'PUT' : 'POST',
      json = JSON.encode(attributes);
  req.onLoad.listen((load_event) {
    var request = load_event.target;
    attributes = JSON.decode(request.responseText);
    if (callback != null) callback(this);
  });
  req.open(method, url);
  req.setRequestHeader('Content-type', 'application/json');
  req.send(json);
}
```

This should start to look quite familiar now. We create an HttpRequest object, open it to POST to the model's url, set the HTTP header as JSON, and send the serialized model attributes. We also establish a request listener that, when it sees a successful load event, will update the model's attributes and invoke the callback, if supplied.

Lastly, we define a very familiar-looking delete() method.

```
delete([callback]) {
  var req = new HttpRequest();
  req.onLoad.listen((load_event) {
    var request = load_event.target;
    if (callback != null) callback(this);
  });
  req.open('delete', url);
  req.send();
}
```

As with Backbone.js, the main means of communication between different parts of the MVC stack are callbacks (or events). Happily, Dart makes callbacks easy, but events even easier—as you'll see when we refactor this in *Events and Streams*. For now, let's move on to building our MVC views!

Hipster Views

Of the three parts to our minimalist MVC library, the view is easily the most lightweight. Sitting atop the MVC stack, it is allowed to communicate directly with either a model or a collection (both at the same time would be frowned upon). Different views will need to list a collection of models, details of individual models, and update models in response to user input. Thus, the view needs to expose both a collection property and a model property. Since it is a view, it also needs an HTML element to which it can attach itself.

The constructor for such a beast looks like the following.

```
class ComicsView {
  var el, model, collection;
  ComicsView({this.el, this.model, this.collection});
}
```

Each of these properties is optional in a view—it will be a collection view subclass's responsibility to know that it is a collection view and, as such, that it needs to access the collection property. Thus, we again make use of Dart's very excellent optional named constructor parameters.

Our view object does not yet fulfill its purpose: rendering to the UI. To actually render the view, a render() method can assign the innerHtml of the view's Element el to the result of applying the template to the collection. In this case, the template does no more than iterate over the entire collection, applying a single comic book template to each model.

```
// ...
render() { el.innerHtml = template(); }

template() =>
  collection.map(_singleComicBookTemplate).join();

_singleComicBookTemplate(comic) => """
    <li id="${comic['id']}">
      ${comic['title']}
      (${comic['author']})
      <a href="#" class="delete">[delete]</a>
    </li>""";
}
```

The template() method is a thing of beauty. We took great pains to make our collection List-like. Those efforts are rewarded here with the map() method, which takes a single argument—a function that is applied to each member of our collection. In this case, we apply the _singleComicBookTemplate() function to each comic book in the collection. Lastly, we join the results of that mapping and we have the template.

Not to be outdone, the _singleComicBookTemplate() private method is an interesting little method. It uses Dart's multiline strings and interpolation to produce a close facsimile of a traditional template.

Surprisingly, that's all that's needed to render the template. Our main() entry point creates a collection object, gives it to the view, and then performs a fetch().

```
main() {
  var comics_view, comics_collection;

  comics_collection = new ComicsCollection(
    onChange: ()=> comics_view.render()
  );
  comics_view = new ComicsView(
    el: document.query('#comics-list'),
    collection: comics_collection
  );
  comics_collection.fetch();
}
```

When fetch() completes, it invokes the supplied callback, at which point the view renders itself.

At this point, we have entirely replicated our original application into an MVC approach. Unlike the original implementation, this approach is aware of how to add and remove items from the back end. Let's add the ability to add a comic book from the collection.

Putting Models, Collections, and Views Together to Create New Records

A true single-page application needs to do more than display a static list of the records in the back end. It should be able to perform all of the usual CRUD operations at a minimum. Let's walk through creating records in the UI to get a feel for how this might work in a Dart MVC-like approach.

Rather than attempt to make our existing ComicsView try to do too much, let's create a new view class for the logic responsible for creating comic book records. In the main() entry point, the new view class can be created after everything else is built.

```
main() {
  var comics_view, comics_collection;


  comics_collection = new ComicsCollection(
    onChange: ()=> comics_view.render()
  );
  comics_view = new ComicsView(
    el: document.query('#comics-list'),
    collection: comics_collection
  );
  comics_collection.fetch();

  new CreateComicView(
    el: document.query('#add-comic'),
    collection: comics_collection
  );
}
```

Given the similarity between the ComicsView and CreateComicView constructors, there is a natural temptation to generalize a single view solution that works for both. We resist this for now, though we give into temptation in Chapter 9, *Project: Extracting Libraries*, on page 85.

Our CreateComicView class needs to attach a click handler for the #add-comic element. When clicked, it should toggle the new comic book form. Our constructor also needs to build that form.

```
class CreateComicView {
  var el, model, collection;
  Element form;

  CreateComicView({this.el, this.model, this.collection}) {
    el.onClick.listen((event) => toggleForm());
    attachForm();
  }
}
```

The Element form is different than in the ComicsView, but we have seen all of this before. Again, the el, model, and collection instance variables are declared as fields in our view. We will also have a form element in this view, which will hold the form. The constructor is defined as always, with the same name as the class. The el, model, and collection instance variables can be optionally set in the constructor.

Different here is that our constructor actually has a body. In addition to simple instance variable assignment, we need to listen for click events to toggle the visibility of the form and to attach the form to the page's DOM.

Toggling the display of the form should look familiar to web programmers. We switch between 'block' and 'none' values for the form's display style.

```
toggleForm() {
  if (form.style.display == 'none') {
    form.style.display = 'block';
  }
  else {
    form.style.display = 'none';
  }
}
```

The real action takes place in the attachForm() method. It creates and adds the form element to the web page, and then adds two event handlers.

```
attachForm() {
  form = new Element.html("<div>${template}</div>");
  form.style.display = 'none';
  el.parent.children.add(form);
  InputElement titleInput = form.query('input[name=title]'),
              authorInput = form.query('input[name=author]');
  // handle create form submission
  form.query('form').onSubmit.listen((event) {
    collection.create({
      'title': titleInput.value,
      'author': authorInput.value
    });
    form.
      queryAll('input[type=text]').
      forEach((InputElement input) => input.value = '');
    toggleForm();
    event.preventDefault();
  });

  // handle clicks on the Cancel link
  form.query('a').onClick.listen((event) {
    toggleForm();
    event.preventDefault();
  });
}
```

The first event handler handles form submission. It extracts the author and title from the form, using them to create a new comic book in the collection. Thanks to all of our previous work, collection.create() not only creates a record in the back end, but it also generates an add event in our MVC stack that ultimately triggers the ComicsView object to add the new record on the web page. The remainder of the form submission handler cleans up and hides the form.

The second handler simply toggles the form when the Cancel link is clicked. Both handlers prevent default actions (form submission, link following) from occurring—our handlers have sufficiently handled the events.

What's Next

Phew! We really put Dart through its paces in this chapter. We took our very first Dart application and converted it to a very functional MVC class approach. We also caught a few glimpses of both object-oriented and event-based programming. At times we glossed over the details of Dart's support for those two programming paradigms, so we will take the next two chapters to explore them in more detail.

When we pick up our project again in *Project: Extracting Libraries*, you'll see one of Dart's absolute coolest early features: real libraries.

CHAPTER 7

Classes and Objects

Chapter 6, *Project: MVC in Dart*, on page 45 made extensive use of classes and objects to build up an MVC library. From this, you can take two lessons: first, it is hard to do significant work in Dart without some object-oriented programming, and second, it is pretty easy to do object-oriented programming in Dart. In this chapter, we will formalize how Dart treats its classes and objects.

Class Is a First-Order Concept

Dart's classical approach to object-oriented programming is a significant, and welcome, departure from JavaScript's prototype-based approach. Prototype-based languages certainly offer some benefits, but ease of approach is not one of them.

As you have seen, Dart classes are introduced with the class keyword.

classes/basics.dart
```
class ComicsCollection {
  // describe class operations here...
}
```

That's all we need in order to define a class in Dart—no fancy constructor functions, no heavy libraries to provide classical classes, just class followed by a class name.

> **Tip**
>
> Although a class is a first-order concept in Dart, it is not a first-order *object*. As you saw in *Project: MVC in Dart*, it is not possible to pass a class name as a variable as we might do in other languages.

Instance Variables

Instance variables are nothing more than variables declared inside a class.

```
class ComicsView {
  ComicsCollection collection;
  ComicModel model;
  Element el;
  // ...
}
```

In this case, we have declared three instance variables of different types. We could have declared all three as having a variable type (var collection, model, el;), but we are being good library maintainers by being explicit about the types.

Instance variables are accessible throughout the class with just their name—there is no need to prepend this. to a variable unless it would help to disambiguate an instance variable from a local variable.

By default, instance variables are public, which means they are accessible by subclasses *and* outside the class. For any public instance variable, Dart automatically creates an external getter and setter with the same name as the instance variable. For example, to access the comic book view's collection, we can do this:

```
comics_view.collection;
// => instance of ComicsCollection
```

To switch the view to a new collection, we can do this:

```
comics_view.collection = new_collection;
```

Public instance variables are a nice convenience but should be used with caution if access control is needed.

Private Instance Variables

In some cases, public instance variables are a scary proposition. If a library does not want to expose an instance variable directly to its consuming context, then it can declare private variables. Private variables in Dart are simply variables that start with an underscore (for example, _models).

If, for example, we did not want to allow the collection to be changed, we could declare the collection as a private instance variable but still expose a public "getter."

```
classes/private.dart
class ComicsView {
  // Private because it starts with underscore
  ComicsCollection _collection;
  ComicsCollection get collection {
    // possibly restrict access here...
    return _collection;
  }
}
```

> **Tip**
>
> Important: Private variables are *only* available in the library in which they are defined. If a subclass is defined in a separate library from its base class, then it cannot access instance variables in the superclass. Similarly, the superclass would not see private instance variables assigned in a subclass. This brings us to a very important rule: *never* access private instance variables between superclass and subclass. It may work when both are in the same library, but if they ever get refactored into separate libraries, bad things will happen. So don't do it. We will run headlong into this restriction in Chapter 11, *Project: Varying Behavior*, on page 103.

Methods

Methods are simply named functions inside a class. The following is a method that renders the current view by assigning the el instance variable's innerHTML to the result of a template.

```
classes/methods.dart
class ComicsView {
  // ...
  render() {
    el.innerHtml = template(collection);
  }
}
```

Inside the class, methods may be invoked by calling the method directly —prepending the method with this. is not required like it is in JavaScript (though it would still work). In the previous example, template() is an instance method that is invoked with the view's collection property.

In Dart, it is generally considered good practice to prepend the return type of a method or prepend void if the method does not return anything.

classes/method_with_type.dart
```
class ComicsView {
  void render() {
    el.innerHtml = template(collection);
  }
}
```

In addition to "normal" methods, Dart supports specialized setter and getter methods as well as operator methods.

Getters and Setters

Getter methods are those that take no arguments and are declared with the keyword get after the type and before the name of the method. They also lack the parentheses of normal methods.

classes/getter_method.dart
```
class ComicsCollection {
  String get url => '/comics';
}
```

Getters get their name from how they are used, which greatly resembles getting an object's property in other languages.

```
// No parens required!
comics_collection.url;        // => '/comics'
```

Dart also supports setters, which are functions that assign new values. These are declared with the set keyword and take the new value as a parameter.

classes/setter_method.dart
```
class ComicsCollection {
  String _url;
  void set url(new_url) {
    _url = new_url;
  }
  String get url => _url;
}
```

Setters are of interest primarily because they override the assignment operator. To set the new URL in the Comics class, we would not pass it as the argument to the url() method. Rather, we assign it.

```
comics_collection.url = shiny_new_url;
```

Dart recognizes assignment as a special setter operation and looks in the class definition for the set keyword to decide how to proceed.

Setters and getters beat the pants off of languages that force us to choose from any number of poor conventions to indicate intent.

Operators

In fact, there are a number of operator-like methods that can be described by a Dart class. The remaining operators are declared with the same keyword: operator.

We saw operator in the ComicModel class as a way to access attributes of the model.

```
classes/operators.dart
class ComicModel {
  Map attributes;
  operator [](attr) => attributes[attr];
}
```

With that, we can then look up the title of a Comic object with the following:

```
comic['title'] // => "V for Vendetta"
```

The square bracket lookup is by far the most common operator in Dart, but a myriad are supported: ==, <, >, <=, >=, -, +, /, ~/, *, %, |, ^, &, <<, >>, []=, [], and ~. Dart's support for operators make it ideal for building math or logic-based libraries or even more fanciful libraries that want to use these operators in their own, unique ways.

The Special, Non-Operator, Non-Getter/Setter, call() Method

There is also a special call() method that lets us describe what should happen when an object is applied. For instance, if we want calling a model (for example, comic()) to be an alias for saving it, we could declare it as follows:

```
classes/call_method.dart
class ComicModel {
  call() {
    save();
  }
  save() {
    // do save things here...
  }
}
```

Then, saving could be accomplished with the following:

```
comic();
```

Between operator methods and the call() method, Dart already supports a very expressive syntax. And it still has more surprises in store for us.

Metaprogramming with **noSuchMethod()**

In its early days, Dart provides for limited metaprogramming facilities. One vehicle for dynamically changing behavior at runtime is the special method noSuchMethod(). When Dart attempts to locate a method being called, it first looks in the current class for the explicit definition. If the method is not located, the superclass and all ancestor classes are checked. Failing that, Dart then invokes noSuchMethod()—if it has been declared—in the current class.

When invoked, noSuchMethod() is supplied with an object that mirrors the method call—an "invocation mirror." This invocation mirror object includes the member (that is, the method) invoked, the list of positional arguments, the list of named arguments, and more.

classes/no_such_method.dart
```
class ComicModel {
  // ...
  noSuchMethod(args) {
    if (args.memberName != new Symbol('save')) {
      throw new NoSuchMethodError(
        this,
        args.memberName,
        args.positionalArguments,
        args.namedArguments
      );
    }
    // Do save operations here...
  }
}
```

We will look into noSuchMethod() in more detail in *Project: Varying Behavior.*

Why Dart Will Not Rush to Become More Dynamic

Dart will likely add more dynamism as it evolves, but it is not a priority for two reasons.

1. It adversely affects code completion.

2. It is a common source of bugs that the compiler cannot identify.

For those of us who are not fans of code completion, #1 is not a strong argument. Ruby and JavaScript programmers might argue with #2—the idea that dynamic language features are a common source of bugs. Even so, they certainly prevent the compiler from catching potential issues.

Regardless, Dart is not opposed to becoming more dynamic in the future; it is just not an immediate priority.

Method Cascades

We already touched on method cascades in Chapter 4, *Manipulating the DOM*, on page 29, but they are worth mentioning again. Cascades are introduced with the double dot operator instead of the usual single dot operator for ordinary methods. Thanks to cascades, we are not stuck adding elements to a list one at a time.

classes/cascades.dart
```
var list1 = [];
list1.add(17);
list1.add(42);
```

Instead, we can add them in a single statement.

```
var list2 = [];
list2
  ..add(17)
  ..add(42);
```

The cascade syntax is meant to evoke the idea of working in Unix directories, where one dot represents the current directory and two dots points to the parent directory. In cascades, two dots refer to the original object receiving the method, not the result of the previous method. This makes for nice, jQuery-like chained code, but for all methods, not just those that operated on jQuery wrapped sets.

A surprising feature of cascades is the support for cascading setters. Setters are, after all, methods in Dart. This allows us, for example, to rewrite a laundry list of style settings.

```
el.style.opacity = '0';
el.style.position = 'absolute';
el.style.top = '80px';
el.style.left = '0px';
el.style.zIndex = '1001';
el.style.transition = 'opacity 1s ease-in-out';
el.style.opacity = '1';
```

That might not look too bad, especially if you are used to performing CSS updates in JavaScript. Compare that to the same functionality, but written in cascades:

```
el.style
  ..opacity = '0'
  ..position = 'absolute'
  ..top = '80px'
  ..left = '0px'
  ..zIndex = '1001'
  ..transition = 'opacity 1s ease-in-out'
  ..opacity = '1';
```

The intent of the code is so much clearer with cascades. It is immediately evident that all of the setters apply to the element's style whereas the old-fashioned way of doing it requires a non-trivial scanning before we can convince ourselves that all setters operate on the same property. Multiply that kind of readability times a hundred or a thousand over a codebase's lifetime, and you will realize some hefty time savings.

Static Methods (aka Class Methods) and Variables

Dart includes the concept of class variables and methods, though it takes a dim view of them. It regards them as a necessary evil, which, of course, they are. These are introduced with the static keyword.

classes/static_methods.dart
```
class Planet {
  static List rocky_planets = const [
    'Mercury', 'Venus', 'Earth', 'Mars'
  ];
  static List gas_giants = const [
    'Jupiter', 'Saturn', 'Uranus', 'Neptune'
  ];
  static List get known {
    var all = [];
    all.addAll(rocky_planets);
    all.addAll(gas_giants);
    return all;
  }
}
```

Invoking a static method is just like invoking an instance method, except the class itself is the receiver.

```
Planet.known
// => ['Mercury', 'Venus', 'Earth', 'Mars',
//     'Jupiter', 'Saturn', 'Uranus', 'Neptune' ]
```

Interestingly, instance methods can treat static methods as if they are other instance methods.

classes/mix_static_and_instance_methods.dart
```
class Planet {
  // ...
  static List get known { ... }
  String name;
  Planet(this.name);
  bool get isRealPlanet =>
    known.any((p) => p == this.name);
}
```

In the previous code, the instance method isRealPlanet invokes the static method known just like it would any instance method. In this way, we can find that Neptune is a real planet but Pluto is not.

```
var neptune = new Planet('Neptune');
var pluto = new Planet('Pluto');

neptune.isRealPlanet      // => true

pluto.isRealPlanet        // => false
```

 Warning: Because Dart treats static methods as instance methods in this fashion, it is illegal to have an instance method with the same name as a class method.

Subclasses

In Dart, we say that a subclass *extends* its superclass with new functionality. As you will see in Chapter 9, *Project: Extracting Libraries*, on page 85, most of a collection's functionality can be factored out into a HipsterCollection superclass. The Comics subclass then needs to extend HipsterCollection with only a few methods.

```
classes/subclasses.dart
class Comics extends HipsterCollection {
  String get url => '/comics';
  HipsterModel modelMaker(attrs) => new ComicBook(attrs);
}
```

The extends keyword has the obvious benefit of reading nicely, which increases a codebase's overall maintainability.

Abstract Methods

In the previous code example, both url and modelMaker are abstract methods in the base class. Abstract methods are just methods without bodies, which should exist only inside explicitly declared abstract classes.

```
abstract class HipsterCollection {
  String get url;
  HipsterModel modelMaker(attrs);
}
```

This indicates that HipsterCollection is an abstract class (that it will not work without a subclass) and is one that ideally overrides these methods. If a subclass does not implement these methods, the code will not throw a compile-time error. However, a not-implemented exception is sure to follow.

Duck-Typing in Dart with implements

Interfaces are programming language constructs that describe at a high level how classes will behave. That is, if a class implements an interface, it must define the methods and instance variables that are declared in the interface.

In Dart, everything is an interface, which is another way of saying that there are no explicit interfaces. Any class in Dart—abstract or concrete—is a potential interface. Our ComicsCollection class could implement the built-in Iterable abstract class.

```
classes/implements.dart
class ComicsCollection implements Iterable {
  void forEach(fn) {
    models.forEach(fn);
  }

  int get length => models.length;
  // ...
}
```

What this tells other Dart classes is that there is a *reasonable* expectation that this class supports Iterable methods like forEach and length. If a class does not implement every method in its interface, Dart will not complain—either at compile-time or runtime. Still, it is bad form and analysis tools like dartanalyzer and the Dart Editor will give you grief.

Dynamic language adherents fancy duck typing, which is the equivalent of asking "Who cares what the type is as long as the object supports forEach?" In fact, Dart will let you get away with this kind of behavior if you like. That said, you are a better Dart citizen if you use an interface to declare *why* you support particular methods.

If you need to support multiple interfaces, simply separate them with commas in the class declaration.

```
classes/implements_multiple.dart
class ComicsCollection implements Iterable, EventTarget {
  // Iterable methods
  void forEach(fn) { /* ... */ }
  int get length { /* ... */ }
  // EventTarget
  Events get on => _on;
  // ...
}
```

To be clear, *none* of this is necessary in Dart, but judicious use of interfaces goes a long way toward improving the readability of code.

Mixins

On occasion, the usual subclass and interface approach to classes is not quite right. One such case occurs so often that Dart supports it directly in the language: mixins. The purpose of mixins is to augment subclassing with additional behavior. This additional behavior is typically something that we will want to reuse in other classes as well.

Consider two simple classes, Person and Animal:

classes/mixins.dart
```
class Person {
  String name;
  Person(this.name);
}

class Animal {
  String name;
  Animal(this.name);
}
```

These two classes are unrelated to each other, though they do share a common name property.

During the course of working with these classes, we decide that we need subclasses of both. The Friend class will extend Person to represent a person with a more intimate relationship. Similarly, the Pet class will extend Animal to encapsulate an animal to which a person might have a special bond.

In both cases, the intimate nature of an implied relationship suggests that we want to be able to warmly greet a Friend or Pet. The greeting will be identical except for the name ("Howdy Alice!" "Howdy Snoopy!"). So the question becomes how do we add this common functionality without duplicating code?

The answer, of course, is with mixins. A mixin is declared as an abstract class. The class is abstract because the class into which it gets mixed will supply some vital information or behavior. In the case of our friends and pets, the corresponding classes will supply the name.

```
abstract class Greeting {
  String get name;
  greet() => "Howdy $name!";
}
```

Our greet() method is fully defined, but the name getter method is left abstract by virtue of being declared without a method body. Both Person and Animal already define this getter by way of a name instance variable. In other words, Greeting is ready to mix in with both classes.

The syntax for mixins works with the extends keyword. In Dart, we say that a class extends another *with* a mixin. So Friend extends Person with Greeting. Pet extends Animal with the same Greeting mixin.

```
class Friend extends Person with Greeting {
  Friend(name): super(name);
}

class Pet extends Animal with Greeting {
  Pet(name): super(name);
}
```

That's all there is to it. Both the Friend and Pet classes now have Greeting's greet() method available for use:

```
var say_hi = new Friend('Alice').greet();
// => 'Howdy Alice!'

var say_hi = new Pet('Snoopy').greet();
// => 'Howdy Snoopy!'
```

Dart expects mixins to work with subclasses. It is possible to mix in traits to top-level classes. In such cases, we would have to extend Object with the mixin. If that seems a little awkward, this is Dart's way of telling us that we might be better off using a subclass in such cases.

Constructors

Dart gets a surprising amount of mileage out of its constructors. It does so through a combination of two types of constructors: generative and factory. The difference between the two has to do with how they create new objects. Generative constructors take care of blessing new objects for us, leaving us the task of initializing the internal state. In a factory constructor, we are responsible for building and returning new objects ourselves. As you will see, there is power in both the simplicity of generative constructors and the flexibility of factory constructors.

Generative constructors are the more common of the two, so we will talk about them first.

Simple Generative Constructors

Borrowing from *Project: MVC in Dart*, the simplest form of a constructor looks a lot like a method with the same name as the class.

```
classes/generative_constructor.dart
class ComicsCollection {
  List<ComicModel> models;
  // Our constructor
  ComicsCollection() {
    models = [];
  }
}
```

The constructor for this class accepts no arguments and sets an instance variable to a default value. There is no return from a generative constructor—we affect only the internal state of an object.

If we only need to set initial values, Dart provides a nice little shorthand. Instead of assigning the initial values in the body of the generative constructor, we can assign them when they are declared.

```
classes/lazy_instance_variable.dart
class ComicsCollection {
  List<ComicModel> models = [];
}
```

Instance variables declared like this are lazily evaluated. That is, they are not actually assigned until an instance of the class is created with the new keyword.

Named Constructors

JavaScript is able to accomplish a lot with the arguments object/array. Accomplishing a lot is another way of saying overloading, which is not conducive to maintainability. Dart takes a more explicit approach to constructor arguments. In addition to optional parameters, which you met in Chapter 3, *Functional Programming in Dart*, on page 21, Dart boasts a neat feature, *named constructors*, which let you create specialized constructors. For instance, if we wanted to be able to create a ComicsCollection from a list of attributes, we could declare a ComicsCollection.fromCollection constructor.

```
classes/named_constructor.dart
class ComicsCollection {
  List<ComicModel> models = [];
  ComicsCollection() {
    // "Normal" constructor here
  }

  ComicsCollection.fromCollection(collection) {
    models = collection.map(
      (attr) => new ComicModel(attr)
    );
  }
}
```

This lets us instantiate a collection object like this:

```
var comics = new ComicsCollection.fromCollection([
  {'id': 1, 'title': 'V for Vendetta', /* ... */ },
  {'id': 2, 'title': 'Superman', /* ... */ },
  {'id': 3, 'title': 'Sandman', /* ... */ }
]);
```

Just like "normal" generative constructors, named constructors begin with the name of the class. The named constructor is denoted with a dot and then the name (for example, .fromCollection). And, just as with other generative constructors, named constructors do not return anything; they merely change the internal state of an object.

Classes can have any number of named constructors in addition to the normal constructor. This allows us to specialize object instantiation through a series of well-named constructors that do one thing. It effectively eliminates the complex conditionals that can plague object initialization in JavaScript.

Named constructors are a *huge* win for readable, maintainable code.

Redirecting Constructors

Once we start making effective use of Dart's multiple constructors, we quickly get into a situation in which we are repeating logic. For instance, two different constructors for the model base class might need to initialize the same attributes instance variable.

classes/ry_constructors.dart
```
class ComicBook {
  Map attributes;
  ComicBook(attrs) {
    this.attributes = attrs;
  }
  ComicBook.named(name) {
    this.attributes = {'title': name};
  }
}
```

To avoid repeating ourselves, we use redirection constructors.

classes/dry_constructors.dart
```
class ComicBook {
  Map attributes;
  ComicBook(attrs) {
    this.attributes = attrs;
  }
  // Redirect from the `named` constructor to the all-purpose constructor
  ComicBook.named(name): this({'title': name});
}
```

Now, the attributes instance variable is assigned in only one place—the default new ComicBook() constructor. That's a nice little maintainability win.

Redirection is introduced with the colon. The target of the redirection follows the colon; in this case, we specify the default constructor with this(). Redirection can point to other named constructors: this.withTitle(title). It can also point to the superclass constructor or named superclass constructors. For instance, the ComicBook model might need to define constructors for more prolific authors.

```
class AwesomeComicBook extends ComicBook {
  AwesomeComicBook(attrs): super(attrs);
  AwesomeComicBook.byNeilGaiman(): this({'author': 'Neil Gaiman'});
  AwesomeComicBook.byAlanMoore(): this({'author': 'Alan Moore'});
}
```

> **Tip**
>
> Important: If no constructors are defined, Dart adopts an implicit this(): super() redirection constructor. As soon as we define any kind of constructor in the subclass—the .byNeilGaiman() constructor in this case—then there is no implied constructor, and we are forced to make the implicit constructor explicit.

Constructor Arguments

You have already seen an example of supplying arguments to named constructors. Regular constructors are no different.

classes/constructor_simple_parameter.dart
```
class ComicBook {
  Map attributes;
  ComicBook(attributes) {
    this.attributes = attributes;
  }
}
```

Dart provides a nice convention for assigning instance variables. Instead of assigning this.attributes in the constructor block as shown earlier, we can declare the parameter as this.attributes.

classes/constructor_this_parameter.dart
```
class ComicBook {
  Map attributes;
  ComicBook(this.attributes);
}
```

This goes a long way toward clearing up intent. Rather than muddying up the assignment of the attributes instance variable alongside other constructor initialization and assignment, the intent is made quite clear in the parameter list. The body of the constructor can then concern itself solely with doing what it needs to in order to create an instance of the class—or can be eliminated entirely as we have done here.

This convention of declaring instance variables in the parameters list even works with optional parameters.

```
classes/constructor_optional_this.dart
class ComicsView {
  ComicsCollection collection;
  ComicModel model;
  Element el;

  ComicsView({this.el, this.model, this.collection}) {
    if (this.el == null) {
      this.el = new DivElement();
    }
  }
}
```

In this case, the constructor has a bit of "real" work to do (building an element if one is not supplied). By declaring this.model and this.collection as optional parameters, the intent of assigning them is clear—without adding clutter to the constructor body.

Optional assignment parameters are passed with the name of the instance variable being assigned.

```
var view = new ComicsView(model: comic_book);
```

Like named constructors, Dart's parameter assignment goes out of its way to help keep your code clean.

Factory Constructors

Dart defines a special class of constructors for returning specialized object instances. The constructors that you have seen so far all manipulate the internal state of the newly created object but leave the blessing of the object and the return value to Dart.

```
class ComicModel {
  ComicModel() {
    attributes = {};
  }

  // ...
}
```

If we instantiate an object via new ComicModel(), then we are returned an object of ComicModel with on and attributes instance variables started in their pristine states. This covers 90 percent of object-oriented programming, but there are times when we might want more.

For instance, what if we do not want to create a new object? What if our class should return a cached copy of a previously assembled object? What if we need our class to always return the same instance? What if we need the constructor to return a different object entirely? Dart defines factory constructors to answer all of those questions. The two syntactic differences between factory and normal constructors are the factory keyword and the return value of the constructor. Consider the factory constructor for the Highlander class.

```
classes/singleton.dart
class Highlander {
  static Highlander the_one;
  String name;

  factory Highlander(name) {
    if (the_one == null) {
      the_one = new Highlander._internal(name);
    }

    return the_one;
  }

  // private, named constructor
  Highlander._internal(this.name);
}
```

The Highlander's factory constructor checks to see whether the class variable the_one has already been defined. If not, it assigns it to a new instance via a private, named constructor and returns the_one. If the_one has already been defined, then no new instance is created, and the previously defined the_one is returned. Thus, we have created a singleton class.

```
var highlander = new Highlander('Connor MacLeod');
var another = new Highlander('Kurgan');
highlander.name;
// => 'Connor MacLeod'
// Nice try Kurgan...
another.name;
// => 'Connor MacLeod'
```

Used wisely, there is much power in these beasties.

What's Next

Dart provides some very nice object-oriented programming features. Most of the emphasis from the language seems to be geared toward making the resulting code cleaner and the intent clearer. Although it supports the this keyword, representing the current object, its use is *far* less prevalent than in JavaScript, and the rules surrounding it far less arcane. Effective use of generative, factory, and redirecting constructors goes a long way toward making our Dart code as clean as possible.

We will revisit classes in *Project: Varying Behavior*. More specifically, there are implications for some of what we discussed that are better brought up in the context of real-world use.

CHAPTER 8

Events and Streams

Regardless of the language, browser events are captured and received and bubble the same way. So, it makes sense that events in Dart behave in a fashion similar to JavaScript...with one very Darty twist.

Plain-Old Events

Consider, for instance, a click handler that colors the border of the clicked element a brilliant orange.

events/simple.dart

```
var el = document.query('#clicky-box');
el.onClick.listen((event) {
  el.style.border = "5px solid orange";
});
```

Here, we define an anonymous function to be invoked when a click event occurs. This is slightly more compact than the equivalent JavaScript code: el.addEventListener('click', callback_fn). But there is a subtle difference in Dart's syntax: the lack of the word "add."

In Dart, the onClick property (like all "on" properties) is a *stream*. That is, the onClick property represents a stream of click events. Every time a DOM element is clicked, the corresponding event is added to the onClick stream and any listeners that are subscribed to receive those events will be invoked.

The difference between a list of callbacks and a stream may seem minor (and really there is not *that* much of a difference). The power of streams comes from their ubiquity in Dart. Anytime there is an event or asynchronous action in Dart, you can find a stream of events or data. There is no need to remember how asynchronous actions behave in the DOM versus how they behave when reading a file—they are the same thing.

In fact, we saw an example of event streams back in Chapter 1, *Project: Your First Dart Application,* on page 3. The onLoad Ajax stream looks like this:

```
events/http_request.dart
req.onLoad.listen((event) {
  var list = JSON.decode(req.responseText);
  container.innerHtml = graphicNovelsTemplate(list);
});
```

It is this kind of organization and consistency that puts the "structured" in Dart's structured code for the modern Web.

In Design Pattern parlance, streams implement a Publish/Subscribe, or pubsub, pattern. The various "on" properties on DOM elements (or anything that describes a stream in Dart) publishes a stream of events. Anything can subscribe to the published stream, via listen(), to get notifications of asynchronous events.

Streams in Dart are almost always read-only. That is, they implement the pubsub pattern and nothing else. Events and data are added to streams by stream controllers such as DOM elements. When it makes sense to allow programmatic generation of stream events, Dart supports helper methods. In the case of DOM elements, for instance, the usual dispatchEvent() DOM method is supported:

```
el.dispatchEvent(new Event('click'));
```

Or, even better, use the built-in click() in Element:

```
el.click();
```

Since streams are pubsub patterns by another name, the listen() method generates a subscription. To unsubscribe from a stream, call the cancel() method on the subscription:

```
var subscription = el.onClick.listen((event) {
  el.style.border = "50px dotted purple";
});
// Do some stuff, then...
subscription.cancel();
```

Subscriptions are also a place to add error handling with onError():

```
var subscription = el.onClick.listen((event) {
  // Normal click handling here...
});
subscription.onError((error) {
  // Add the error to the list of errors...
  errors.add(error);
});
```

One of the cooler features of Dart streams is that they are iterable. This means that they implement Iterable methods like distinct(), takeWhile(), and even where():

```
// Only count clicks where the Control key is also held down:
el.onClick.
  where((e)=> e.ctrlKey).
  listen((event) {
    clicked++;
  });
```

There is a lot of power in Dart streams, so let's spend some time in the next section to build our own.

Making Custom Events with Streams

Dart includes dozens of event streams in the dart:html library alone. In addition to the MouseEvent stream that we have already explored, Dart has streams for everything from Ajax events to application cache events. But sometimes that is not enough.

As mentioned in the previous section, Dart streams do not expose a way to add events or data. It might seem as though streams are useless should we want a stream on which other code can listen for our custom events. Well, streams are far from useless. In this case we need a StreamController.

Revisiting the ComicsCollection class, we have already briefly seen custom "on" properties like onLoad and onAdd.

events/collection_events.dart

```
class ComicsCollection extends IterableBase {
  StreamController _onLoad = new StreamController.broadcast(),
                  _onAdd = new StreamController.broadcast();

  List models = [];
  // ...
}
```

The _onLoad and _onAdd stream controllers allow us to dispatch events to the underlying streams. The stream controllers are constructed as broadcast streams because streams are "shy" by default. Unless we explicitly tell our stream controllers that they are broadcast, then the pubsub is a single subscription only.

With broadcast streams, we can listen with as many callbacks as we desire.

```
hipster_collection.onAdd
  ..listen((model) { /* listener #1 */ })
  ..listen((model) { /* listener #2 */ })
  ..listen((model) { /* listener #3 */ });
```

Let's take a look at the actual "event" being generated on our streams. This turns out to be as simple as can be: anything can be placed on a stream. Nothing really stops us from adding strings, integers, and dates onto the same stream controller:

```
stream_controller.add('Hi Bob!');
stream_controller.add(42);
stream_controller.add(new DateTime.now());
```

Typically streams only support one kind of object. In other words, we deal with a stream of strings, a stream of integers, or a stream of browser events. To advertise what gets published on a particular stream, streams can be defined with a specialized type declaration called "generics." To declare that a Stream will only contain comic book model classes, declare the normal Stream type followed immediately by the contained type in angle brackets:

```
Stream<ComicModel> get onLoad => _onLoad.stream;
Stream<ComicModel> get onAdd => _onAdd.stream;
```

As with any other type definition in Dart, that will not catch runtime errors. It does provide some very clear documentation for others to follow. Plus, the dartanalyzer or Dart Editor will warn you if you ever try to treat objects in those streams as anything other than a ComicModel.

The ComicsCollection base class publishes its events on these streams by adding them to the stream controller. For instance, when a new model is added to the collection, we add it to the list of models and to the _onAdd stream controller.

```
class ComicsCollection extends IterableBase {
  // ...
  add(model) {
    models.add(model);
    _onAdd.add(model);
  }
}
```

To react to collection events, the Comics view collection need only listen to the stream in exactly the same way that any stream anywhere in Dart is listening.

```
class ComicsView {
  // called by the constructor
  _subscribeEvents() {
    if (collection == null) return;
    collection.onLoad.listen((event)=> render());
    collection.onAdd.listen((event)=> render());
  }
}
```

Just like that, the view renders itself when the collection is loaded from the back-end data store or whenever a new item is added to the collection.

The main benefit of evented approaches like this is an elegant separation of concerns. The collection doesn't need to know anything of the view. The collection merely dispatches its events during the normal course of its work—blissfully unaware that the view is desperate for its notifications so that it can redraw itself immediately.

Best of all, we are using streams to accomplish this. No matter what kind of Dart code there is, it will be using streams, so there is no need to learn something new for server-side Dart or HTTP request Dart. It is all streams!

What's Next

Dart exposes a rich eventing system that runs the gamut of developer needs. There are UIEvent, HTTP ProgressEvent, FileSystemEvent, and many more classes. Because they sport a familiar API, they're easy to use and intuitive. And, when these simpler mechanisms aren't enough, Dart makes it easy to define your own event systems.

In Chapter 14, *Futures and Isolates*, on page 127, we will discuss another means for separate chunks of code to communicate. In both cases, a little ceremony goes a long way toward keeping code well factored and maintainable.

Part III

Code Organization

Now that you've had your first taste of Dart's power, we'll check out something truly unique to Dart: the library system. Previously, we treated the MVC library that we're building as if we were still limited to JavaScript. That is, we put everything into one large file. Dart comes with a sophisticated built-in library system. As you'll see, this means that writing large libraries is not only possible but easy.

CHAPTER 9

Project: Extracting Libraries

Back in Chapter 6, *Project: MVC in Dart*, on page 45, we rewrote our simple Dart application in an MVC style similar to the venerable Backbone.js. As is, there is little possibility for reuse of this code—either in our own codebase or shared with others.

In this chapter, we will factor those MVC classes into reusable libraries. This involves two separate activities: putting our newfound object-oriented Dart skills to use and making use of Dart's excellent library system. The end results will facilitate both code reuse as well as better code maintainability.

Also in this chapter, you'll run into something that you won't find in most language books: some actual limitations of the language being discussed.

What to Extract and What to Leave

For each of the collection, model, and view classes from *Project: MVC in Dart*, we are now faced with the question of what to extract.

Collections: Everything but the Hard Stuff

As we did in *Project: MVC in Dart*, we start with the core of the client-side MVC library: the collection. Since collections are loose code mappings to a REST-like back end, we ought to be able to extract much of ComicsCollection into a HipsterCollection superclass. Anything that is specific to comics books, such as the */comics* URL, can stay in ComicsCollection. The rest (ideally) can move out to be reused with other REST-like back ends.

With everything else in HipsterCollection, ComicsCollection can be expressed as follows:

```
class ComicsCollection extends HipsterCollection {
  // url => the url root of the collection
  // other comics book specific methods, if any
}
```

If we move everything in HipsterCollection, our starting point looks like this:

mvc_library/test/collection_skel.dart
```
class HipsterCollection extends IterableBase {
  // Lazily evaluated instance variables
  StreamController _onLoad, _onAdd;
  var models = [];

  // MVC
  fetch() { /* ... */ }
  create(attrs) { /* ... */ }
  add(model) { /* ... */ }

  // Iterable
  Iterator get iterator => models.iterator;
}
```

Aside from renaming the constructor to HipsterCollection(), very little else needs to change. In fact, the only changes that are required involve the URL, which we planned for, and the create() method, which can no longer hard-code new ComicsBook() in order to generate models.

To indicate that an instance variable like url should be defined in a Dart subclass, we declare the getter and setter as abstract. That is, we define them without method bodies inside of an abstract class.

mvc_library/test/superclass_access_to_subclass_ivar.dart
```
abstract class HipsterCollection extends IterableBase {
  void set url(v);
  String get url;

  fetch() {
    // HTTP Request url from subclass
  }

  // ...
}
```

This tells Dart's typing system that any concrete subclass must define the url instance variable.

```
class ComicsCollection extends HipsterCollection {
  var url = '/comics';
}
```

With that, the fetch() method in the HipsterCollection base class will be able to determine which URL it needs to request.

With the URL out of the way, let's see how the concrete class tells the super-class how to build models. This turns out to be trickier than the url() getter.

In Backbone.js, for instance, the class that creates models is conveyed by a property.

```
mvc_library/old/backbone_sub_class.js
var Comics = Backbone.Collection.extend({
  model: ComicBook
});
```

This will not work in Dart because classes are not first-order objects. That is, there is no way to assign a class name to a variable or use one as the value of a Hash/Map. So, we have to settle for a factory method that, given model attributes, will return a new instance of the model that we desire. That is, we add a modelMaker() method.

```
mvc_library/test/model_maker_method.dart
class ComicsCollection extends HipsterCollection {
  var url = '/comics';
  modelMaker(attrs) => new ComicBook(attrs);
}
```

Back in the HipsterCollection superclass, we declare modelMaker() as abstract (by omitting the method body) and update create() to use this method.

```
abstract class HipsterCollection extends IterableBase {
  HipsterModel modelMaker(Map attrs);
  // ...
  create(attrs) {
    var new_model = modelMaker(attrs);
    new_model.save(callback:(event) {
      this.add(new_model);
    });
  }
  // ...
}
```

That is a bit of a hassle compared to the Backbone.js pass-a-class approach. Still, it is not *too* bad.

The limitation is a simple question of priorities. The Dart designers favored defining a well-structured, classical, object-oriented paradigm over treating classes as first-order objects. They favored strongly encapsulated instance variables over shared definitions between classes. And their choices seem to be well supported given that our "workaround" is a one-liner.

The Model: Nothing to See Here

The implementation of the HipsterModel class is even simpler—everything goes there, leaving a subclass to do nothing other than redirecting the constructor.

```
mvc_library/test/model.dart
class ComicBook extends HipsterModel {
  ComicBook(attributes) : super(attributes);
  get urlRoot => '/comics';
}
```

We have the bother of explicitly passing the subclass constructor arguments to the superclass. Aside from that, the HipsterModel base class takes care of everything (recall that the url comes from the collection).

If instances of HipsterModel are ever used directly, then our subclass would need to override the urlRoot getter as we have done here.

This is not to suggest that HipsterModel is simple. It is still responsible for updating and deleting records, as well as generating events for which collections and views can listen. Still, there are no surprises or complications when we extract the code out of ComicBook and put it in HipsterModel.

Views and Post-initialization

One of the shortcomings of the optional constructor syntax is that we need to explicitly delegate it in subclasses.

```
mvc_library/test/view.dart
class ComicBookView extends HipsterView {
  ComicBookView({el, model, collection}):
    super(el:el, model:model, collection:collection);
}
```

Okay, it is not *that* much of a bother, but it would be nice if future versions of Dart could shrink that to a single line.

The base class remains blessedly simple, declaring instance variables and a constructor that optionally sets them.

```
class HipsterView {
  var el, model, collection;
  HipsterView({this.el, this.model, this.collection});
}
```

Views need to be able to listen for model and collection events, but this is a very subclass-dependent definition. To accommodate this, we can attach handlers and subscribe to events in the subclass's constructor, after setting the appropriate instance variables in the superclass first.

```
class ComicsListing extends HipsterView {
  ComicsListing({el, model, collection}):
    super(el:el, model:model, collection:collection) {
    _attachUiHandlers();
    _subscribeEvents();
  }
}
```

The private _subscribeEvents() and _attachUiHandlers() methods are the same from *Project: MVC in Dart*; they are event handlers that render the comic book collection on the screen and delegate UI event handlers for deleting comic books from the collection. In both cases, they are specific to our Dart Comics application, not the Hipster MVC library.

Real Libraries

Our main.dart is getting awfully crowded at this point. We have the main() entry point, HipsterCollection, HipsterModel, HipsterView, and the various concrete classes. It's too large to maintain easily and too entwined to let us reuse code.

To solve both problems, we move classes out into separate files. We will use Dart's built-in library support to make this transition both smooth and well positioned for future reuse and maintainability.

Beginning with HipsterCollection, let's create HipsterCollection.dart. To make this a proper Dart library, we need to start with the library directive. We also need to import the necessary core packages explicitly required by HipsterCollection.

mvc_library/public/scripts/HipsterCollection.dart
```
library hipster_collection;
import 'dart:html';
import 'dart:async';
import 'dart:collection';
import 'dart:convert';
import 'HipsterModel.dart';

abstract class HipsterCollection extends IterableBase {
  StreamController _onLoad = new StreamController.broadcast(),
                  _onAdd = new StreamController.broadcast();

  List models = [];
  HipsterModel modelMaker(attrs);
  String get url;
  // Other hip collection stuff goes here...
}
```

When we pull the ComicsCollection class out into its own ComicsCollection.dart file, it too needs an opening library statement. It also needs to pull in HipsterCollection so that it can subclass it. Defining a subclass of the HipsterCollection base class is a matter of extending HipsterCollection and defining those two abstract methods. It should look something like this:

mvc_library/public/scripts/Collections.Comics.dart
```dart
library comics_collection;
import 'HipsterCollection.dart';
import 'Models.ComicBook.dart';
class Comics extends HipsterCollection {
  get url => '/comics';
  modelMaker(attrs) => new ComicBook(attrs);
}
```

> **Tip**
>
> I find it best to use a bit of Hungarian notation in my MVC filenames (for example, Models.ComicBook.dart and Collections.Comic-Book.dart), but *not* in the class names themselves because that can make code very noisy.

We defer the details of the library directive until the next chapter. It is extremely powerful. Our last word on the matter in this chapter will be to look at what happens to the main.dart entry point after everything else is pulled out into separate library files.

mvc_library/public/scripts/comics.dart
```dart
import 'Collections.Comics.dart' as Collections;
import 'Views.Comics.dart' as Views;
main() {
  var my_comics_collection = new Collections.Comics(),
      comics_view = new Views.Comics(
        el: '#comics-list',
        collection: my_comics_collection
      );
  my_comics_collection.fetch();
}
```

We instantiate a comics collection and pass that and the DOM ID of the unordered list to the view constructor. Finally, we fetch the collection and allow the various events to trigger the view to render itself when appropriate.

Note the as option on the import statements. To keep the code as clean as possible, both the Comics view collection and the Comics collection proper were defined with a class name of Comics.

```dart
// Collections.Comics.dart
class Comics extends HipsterCollection { /* ... */}

// Views.Comics.dart
class Comics extends HipsterView { /* ... */ }
```

It would seem overly wordy to declare the view, for instance, as ComicsView extends HipsterView. But when both are used in the same context, there's the very real problem of colliding class definitions. This is where Dart's as option for import is extremely handy.

By importing Collections.Comics.dart with the Collections prefix, all top-level class definitions are now referenced with the Collections.* prefix. That is, to instantiate a collection object, we use new Collections.Comics(). That's a huge help with code organization, especially when working with applications that define numerous libraries (as is typical in MVC applications).

> **Tip** For the curious, the final version of our Hipster MVC library is located at https://github.com/eee-c/hipster-mvc/.

What's Next

We put our object-oriented knowledge from Chapter 7, *Classes and Objects*, on page 59 to some good use here. Along the way, we exposed a few of Dart's warts. It is not possible, for instance, to pass class names as we would variables. It is not possible to define an instance variable in a subclass so that the superclass can see it. It is not possible for a superclass to access private methods of a subclass. Even though some of these realities may fly in the face of what we might expect in object-oriented code, Dart has some good reasons for this, as we will explore in upcoming chapters.

Regardless of the restrictions, we also found some fairly unobtrusive workarounds. And by workarounds, I mean "The Dart Way." Better still, our object-oriented refactoring put us in a good position to make use of Dart's very cool library system.

Code reuse and maintainability are seemingly impossible challenges to master in the browser, and yet Dart handles libraries with ease. By factoring our MVC library and classes out into their own files, we make it easy to find and maintain specific aspects of our codebase. At the same time, we have sacrificed none of the ease of working with the code; aside from the introduction of a few import and library statements, our code is unchanged from when it was all in one big file.

In the next chapter, we will take a look at libraries in a little more depth and then discuss part, the cousin to import. When we pick back up with our project in Chapter 11, *Project: Varying Behavior*, on page 103, we will adapt it for use with local storage.

CHAPTER 10

Libraries

JavaScript has been around for 18 years. In all that time, it still lacks a simple library loading mechanism. This is not for lack of need. There are many independent solutions and even several attempts at standards (commonjs, AMD, and ECMAscript harmony modules).[1,2,3] As these standards have languished in various states of usefulness and adoption, the community has generated more loader plugins than can be counted.

Despite all of these efforts, the surest way to load additional JavaScript libraries is via a combination of additional <script> tags and compressing multiple files into a single compressed JavaScript script. Neither solution is without problems (such as load order and deployment complexity).

Mercifully, Dart has the concept of libraries built in. Better yet, they are very easy to work with. Dart currently supports two different vehicles for importing functionality into Dart code: part and import.

Parts

The part directive is used to include arbitrary chunks of Dart code into the current context. Consider, for instance, a library that has clearly grown too big for its britches, the simple_multiples library.

libraries/simple_multiples.dart
```
library simple_multiples;
quadruple_triple_double(x) => 4 * triple_double(x);
triple_double(x) => 3 * double(x);
double(x) => 2 * x;
```

1. http://wiki.commonjs.org/
2. https://github.com/amdjs/amdjs-api/wiki/AMD
3. http://wiki.ecmascript.org/doku.php?id=harmony:modules

Okay. No one in their right mind would want to split such a simple library into parts, but hipsters aren't necessarily in their right mind. So let's pull this library apart just to see how we might do it.

To really explore parts, we leave the double() method in the current library and move the other two methods out into their own files. Our simple_multiples.dart would now look like the following:

libraries/sum_of_parts.dart
```
library simple_multiples;
part 'quadruple_triple_double.dart';
part 'triple_double.dart';
double(x) => 2 * x;
```

If this looks like an exact copy of the original library, that's by design. The part directives insert the contents of the referenced files directly into this library as if they never left.

The parts themselves do require a bit more ceremony than just straight code extraction. The parts *must* be declared as part of a library. This is done with the part of directive.

libraries/triple_double.dart
```
part of simple_multiples;
triple_double(x) => 3 * double(x);
```

Here, we have declared that this "part" will be used as part of the simple_multiples library—and *only* the simple_multiples library.

The quadruple_triple_double.dart part is then declared in the same format.

libraries/quadruple_triple_double.dart
```
part of simple_multiples;
quadruple_triple_double(x) => 4 * triple_double(x);
```

In order for the quadruple_triple_double() method to work, it needs access to the triple_double() method, which is defined in a separate part. And the triple_double() method is dependent on the double() method, which is defined in the main library. It should be clear that, for this to work, all parts are considered to be part of the library's namespace and runtime. Any of the parts has access to all other parts *and* the main library as if they were all designed in the same file.

In Dart, we will not normally factor out functions as we have done here. The real power of parts is the ability to split classes out into separate files. There is no need to define HipsterCollection, CollectionEvents, CollectionEventList, and so forth in the same file. Each can go in separate part files. This is a *huge* win for code organization and maintainability.

Libraries

Of more interest is the import statement, which allows us to import classes for use in our code. From the start, Dart supports this feature that comes standard in all server-side languages. Better still, it works transparently in the browser.

As with the part statement, the source file that is being imported requires the library statement at the top of the file. In both cases, the library statement introduces an isolated scope for the code defined within. Consider, for example, a pretty-printing stopwatch class that might be used to time code.

libraries/pretty_stop_watch.dart
```dart
library pretty_stop_watch;

class PrettyStopwatch {
  Stopwatch timer = new Stopwatch();

  PrettyStopwatch.running() {
    timer = new Stopwatch()..start();
  }
  start() {
    timer.start();
  }
  stop() {
    timer.stop();
    print("Elapsed time: ${timer.elapsedMilliseconds} ms");
  }
}
```

The name in the library statement is used in the output of the dartdoc documentation and in the comments of compiled JavaScript. It also serves as a nice form of documentation.

If we wanted to time how long it took to count to 10 million, we would use our pretty stopwatch like this:

libraries/time_counting.dart
```dart
import 'pretty_stop_watch.dart';

main() {
  var timer = new PrettyStopwatch.running();
  for(var i=0; i<10000000; i++) {
    // just counting
  }
  timer.stop();
}
```

As nice as the part statement is, the import statement has much more potential for helping to organize our code. Not only is Dart strongly object-oriented, but it makes it dirt easy to share and reuse class libraries, even in the browser.

> **Tip**
>
> Note: Chrome, or rather Dartium, is smart enough to load part and import files only once, no matter how many different places they might be referenced.

Prefixing Imports

The import statement allows us to namespace imported classes. Even though we typically import only the classes that we need directly in Dart code, there is still the very real possibility for name collision.

Consider, for example, the case in which our MVC application needs the Comics collection as well as the Comics view. Both would be declared as class Comics (although they would extend HipsterCollection and HipsterView). If we attempt to import them directly, Dart's compiler throws an already-defined exception.

To get around this potential limitation, we prefix the imports.

libraries/prefixed_imports.dart
```
library prefixed_imports;

import 'collections/Comics.dart' as Collections;
import 'views/Comics.dart' as Views;
import 'views/AddComic.dart' as Views;
```

With that, we no longer reference the Comics view class or the Comics collection class. Instead, we use Views.Comics and Collections.Comics.

```
main() {
  var my_comics_collection = new Collections.Comics(),
      comics_view = new Views.Comics(
        el:document.query('#comics-list'),
        collection: my_comics_collection
      );
}
```

The implication of prefixes is that there is no global object namespace in Dart. The main() entry point has its own isolated workspace, with its own classes and objects. The various libraries that are imported all have their own object namespace. This cuts down on much of the ceremony involved with code organizing and is another way that Dart encourages us to write clean code.

Core Dart Libraries

Dart defines a set of core libraries, the documentation for which is always publicly available at http://api.dartlang.org. At the time of this writing, many of the libraries are still undergoing active development. The important ones are:

dart:core

> Contains core data types (no need to import this library, it is automatically imported into all Dart applications).

dart:html

> For use in browser applications. Includes things like Element and HttpRequest.

dart:io

> For use in server-side applications. Includes things like File and Server.

dart:async

> Useful when writing applications that need custom streams and futures.

dart:convert

> For use when converting between JSON and native types as well as character encoding.

And that's just scratching the surface. There are libraries for WebGL, cryptography, collections, logging, code mirroring, and isolates. Each library defines a number of common classes that we might want to make use of in our applications.

To use one of these core libraries, we use the import statement just like we would do for our own defined libraries.

```
import 'dart:html';
import 'dart:convert';
```

Packaging with Dart Pub

The Dart SDK already includes the nifty little package management tool named pub, which is capable of resolving and installing dependencies. The Dart pub command can install packages from a central repository, publicly available Git repositories, or even your local filesystem.

The most common pub action is installing an application's dependencies. The pub get command will do this, but it needs a YAML configuration file first.

If we are so set in our JavaScript ways, we might want JSON.stringify() and JSON.parse() instead of the encode/decode methods that are built into the internal dart:convert library. The json package, which is available on the central pub.dartlang.org repository, does just that. The pubspec.yaml configuration for an old-timey JSON application might look something like this:

```
libraries/pub/pubspec.yaml
name: old_timey_json
description: In my day JSON stringified!
dependencies:
  json: any
```

Only the name is required (a description is always nice), but there is not much point to a pubspec.yaml without package dependencies. The any property for the json package means that we will accept any version of the library, which defaults to the most recent.

With just that, it is possible to retrieve the json package for use in your application with pub get.

```
$ pub get
Resolving dependencies......
Downloading json 0.8.7 from hosted...
Got dependencies!
```

If you suspect that your dependencies have gotten out of date, the pub upgrade will check for the latest versions of your dependencies and install them for you. The Dart Editor, of course, has menu options for pub dependency retrieval.

Are you ready for maybe the coolest thing about Dart? Trust me, this is amazing. To use your newly installed packages in code, you import them like this:

```
import 'package:json/json.dart';
```

What's so cool about that? It works on the server-side *and* in the browser. No hoops to jump through. No nested functions that obscure application code with dependencies. Just install your dependencies and import them. And it just works. Was I right?

There are two ways to lock dependencies with pub. The first is to do nothing. The pub get command writes a pubspec.lock with the version number of all packages installed. Future uses of pub get will use the same versions. This is the preferred option for applications. The more explicit approach is to replace any with a specific version number in pubspec.yaml. That's the preferred option if you are publishing your library for others to use.

Speaking of publishing your libraries, it is quite easy. Your pubspec.yaml will need a few more properties (like author and version). It will also need to follow a package convention (for starters, your tests go in the test subdirectory and your code goes in the lib subdirectory). The http://pub.dartlang.org site contains lots of good information. Best of all, you can always pub lish (pub...lish, get it?) and, before asking you to authenticate via OAuth, pub will give you some helpful hints about where you might better follow the conventions.

All of this adds up to something very special. It is a reach to call this revolutionary since programmers have had access to modules, libraries, and packages management for almost as long as long as we have had programming. Even JavaScript has various *partial* solutions (Browserify, RequireJS, Bower). But the ability to do all of this cleanly in the browser, where it has not been possible for the nearly 20 years of browser programming...that very much has the feel of a revolutionary feature.

What's Next

The built-in ability to organize code is a significant win for Dart. The lightweight syntax that Dart employs ensures that we no longer have an excuse for messy client-side application codebases. Let's take a look next at some other Dart features that are ideal for maintaining large applications.

Part IV

Maintainability

Hot on the heels of learning how to organize Dart code, you'll next explore strategies for keeping code maintainable. First, we'll update the Hipster MVC library to accommodate multiple methods of syncing data with a remote (or even local) back end. Then, we'll look at one of Dart's newer features: testing.

CHAPTER 11

Project: Varying Behavior

Those of us coming from a dynamic language background expect to be able to perform all manner of crazy hackery at runtime. Not satisfied with changing a response based on state, we like to change implementation.

In JavaScript, for instance, it is possible to replace the method on an object's prototype at any time. In Ruby, we can replace a function with a lambda. We revel in metaprogramming and cry foul when newbies look at it as magic.

In Dart, there are far fewer opportunities for magic. But it is still possible. To explore this topic, we again return to our comic book catalog application. This time, we will replace the Ajax back-end calls with in-browser storage.

Vary Class Behavior with noSuchMethod()

We first met noSuchMethod() in Chapter 7, *Classes and Objects*, on page 59. Let's try to put it to use as a means for switching the behavior of the save() method in the Hipster MVC library. We already have it saving to a REST-like back end. Let's get it saving to either REST-like storage or localStorage.

Recall that when HipsterModel invokes save(), it sends a JSON representation of its attributes to the REST-like data store and establishes handlers for successful updates.

```
mvc_library/public/scripts/HipsterModel.dart
class HipsterModel {
  // ...
  save({callback}) {
    var req = new HttpRequest();
    req.onLoad.listen((event) {
      attributes = JSON.decode(req.responseText);
      _onSave.add(this);
      if (callback != null) callback(this);
    });
```

```
    req.open('post', urlRoot);
    req.setRequestHeader('Content-type', 'application/json');
    req.send(json);
  }
  String get json => JSON.encode(attributes);
}
```

To successfully replace this with a local storage implementation, we need to save locally and ensure that the same callbacks are called and that the same events are dispatched. To save a model in localStorage, we might create a sub-class that overwrites an in-memory copy of the database with the new or updated model and saves the entire database.

varying_the_behavior/public/scripts/Models.LocalComic.dart
```
class LocalComic extends HipsterModel {
  LocalComic(attributes) : super(attributes);

  save({callback}) {
    var id = (attributes['id'] != null) ?
      attributes['id'] : hashCode.toString();

    var json = window.localStorage[urlRoot],
        data = (json != null) ? JSON.decode(json) : {};

    attributes['id'] = id;
    data[id] = attributes;

    window.localStorage[urlRoot] = JSON.encode(data);

    if (callback != null) callback(data);
  }

  //...
}
```

We'll worry about the details of localStorage later.

So far, we have replaced the Ajax implementation with a localStorage version of save in *a single subclass*. What happens when we need to do the same for another model? What about deletes?

Recall from *Classes and Objects* that noSuchMethod() is a last resort for Dart if it is unable to locate an invoked method anywhere. Instead of the pain of creating a series of subclasses, we can use noSuchMethod() in the HipsterModel base class.

Dart invokes noSuchMethod() with an object that describes the method called and the parameters supplied. The first thing that any noSuchMethod() implementation should do is guard for the known methods that it is capable of handling.

```
varying_the_behavior/test/no_such_method_guard.dart
class HipsterModel {
  // ...
  noSuchMethod(args) {
    if (args.memberName != #save) {
      return super.noSuchMethod(args);
    }
    // ...
  }
}
```

If anything other than the save() method has been invoked, we let the super-class handle things, possibly throwing an exception if no superclasses support the method. The memberName that describes the method being invoked is a Dart symbol. The pound sign is syntactic sugar for const Symbol('save'). Both describe a constant that is guaranteed to be identical to any other use of the same value, making them ideal for use as identifiers. In this case, the symbol identifies the method name being called.

> **Tip**
>
> Note: It is a bit of a pain to work up the class ancestry chain with noSuchMethod(). If the ComicBook model uses noSuchMethod() to perform a bit of unrelated metaprogramming but wants to allow the noSuchMethod() in the HipsterModel base class to handle saves, the subclass has a bit of manual work to do. Specifically, it must manually return the result of invoking super.noSuch-Method(args), where args is the object supplied to noSuchMethod().

With the guard in place, we are ready to invoke either the local storage save or the Ajax save. The naïve approach would be to pass the arguments directly to the two private methods that hold this behavior.

```
varying_the_behavior/test/calling_methods_from_no_such_method.dart
class HipsterModel {
  bool useLocal;
  // ...
  noSuchMethod(args) {
    // Guard clauses here ...

    if (useLocal) {
      // THIS WON'T WORK
      _localSave(args);
    }
    else {
```

```
      // THIS WON'T WORK
      _ajaxSave(args);
    }
  }
  _localSave({callback}) { /* ... */ }
  _ajaxSave({callback}) { /* ... */ }
}
```

This fails, however, because _localSave() and _ajaxSave() expect only optional, named parameters. Here, we are passing our args object, which is an Invocation-Mirror. Our only resort is to manually extract the arguments and place them in the appropriate parameter position.

varying_the_behavior/test/ugly_no_such_method.dart
```
class HipsterModel {
  bool useLocal;
  final CB = const Symbol('callback');
  // ...
  noSuchMethod(args) {
    // Guard clauses here...
    if (useLocal) {
      _localSave(callback: args.namedArguments[CB]);
    }

    else {
      _ajaxSave(callback: args.namedArguments[CB]);
    }
  }
  _localSave({callback}) { /* ... */ }
  _ajaxSave({callback}) {
    // Save over HTTP, then invoke callback...
    if (callback != null) callback(new Event('Save'));
  }
}
```

Thanks to the ability to extract named (and positional) parameters from args, it is possible to achieve a certain amount of flexibility in noSuchMethod(). Ultimately, this will prove to be a poor approach for our MVC library due to the number of places that would require such conditionals. We would need to account for CRUD operations in both model and collection. Let's take a look at a better approach next.

Sync Through Dependency Injection

We need a mechanism to inject a syncing behavior that can be shared between model and collection. Let's create a HipsterSync class that holds our data syncing behavior. Ultimately, the various libraries that rely on HipsterSync will invoke a static method HipsterSync.send() to dispatch the CRUD operation. Before looking at that, however, we need a default behavior that can perform Ajax requests.

```
varying_the_behavior/public/scripts/HipsterSync.dart
library hipster_sync;
import 'dart:html';
import 'dart:convert';

class HipsterSync {
  static _defaultSync(method, model, {options}) {
    var req = new HttpRequest();
    _attachCallbacks(req, options);

    req.open(method, model.url);

    // POST and PUT HTTP request bodies if necessary
    if (method == 'post' || method == 'put') {
      req.setRequestHeader('Content-type', 'application/json');
      req.send(JSON.encode(model.attributes));
    }
    else {
      req.send();
    }
  }

}
```

That all looks fairly normal now that we have taken the initial Ajax-based app and converted it to an MVC framework. We create an HttpRequest object, open it, and then send the request. New here is the need to support passing request bodies with POST and PUT requests, but a simple conditional suffices to cover this behavior.

All of the classes that will use this sync need to be able to dispatch events upon successful load of the HttpRequest object. The _attachCallbacks() static method takes care of this for us.

```
class HipsterSync {
  static _defaultSync(method, model, {options}) {
    var req = new HttpRequest();
    _attachCallbacks(req, options);

  // ...
}

  static _attachCallbacks(request, options) {
    if (options == null) return;
    if (options.containsKey('onLoad')) {
      request.onLoad.listen((event) {
        var req = event.target,
            json = JSON.decode(req.responseText);
```

```
      options['onLoad'](json);
    });
  }
  }
}
```

This _attachCallbacks() method lets us rewrite HipsterModel#save() with an onLoad callback passed via options.

varying_the_behavior/public/scripts/HipsterModel.dart
```
library hipster_model;
import 'HipsterSync.dart';

class HipsterModel {

  // ...
  save({callback}) {
    HipsterSync.send('post', this, options: {
      'onLoad': (attrs) {
        attributes = attrs;
        if (callback != null) callback(this);
      }
    });
  }
}
```

With that, we have delegated data syncing to HipsterSync—the model no longer knows anything about HTTP. The first two arguments to HipsterSync.send() instruct the sync that it should POST when syncing and that the current model should be used to obtain the serialized data to be sent to the back-end store.

At this point, we're finally ready to look at HipsterSync.send(). As we'd expect, if no alternative sync strategy has been supplied, it invokes a _defaultSync().

```
class HipsterSync {
  // ...
  static send(method, model, {options}) {
    if (_injected_sync == null) {
      return _defaultSync(method, model, options:options);
    }
    else {
      return _injected_sync(method, model, options:options);
    }
  }
}
```

The interesting behavior is that _injected_sync beastie. It may look like another static method, but it is, in fact, a class variable. User libraries can inject behavior into this library via a sync= setter, which expects a function.

```
varying_the_behavior/old/hipster_sync_injected.dart
class HipsterSync {
  static var _injected_sync;
  static set sync(fn) {
    _injected_sync = fn;
  }
  static send(method, model, [options]) {
    if (_injected_sync == null) {
      return _defaultSync(method, model, options:options);
    }
    else {
      return _injected_sync(method, model, options:options);
    }
  }
  // ...
}
```

The injected function will need to accept the same arguments that _defaultSync()
does.

> **Tip**
>
> Warning: It would make more sense to have a sync setter *and*
> a sync class method. Unfortunately, Dart will throw an "already
> defined" internal error if a method is declared with the same
> name as a setter. Hence, we need to declare a sync= setter and
> a send static method.

With all of this in place, let's switch our HipsterSync strategy to localStorage. This
can be done back in the main() entry point for the application. For now, we
restrict ourselves to supporting only the GET operations.

```
varying_the_behavior/old/main_with_local_sync.dart
import 'HipsterSync.dart';
main() {
  HipsterSync.sync = localSync;
  // Setup collections and views ...
}
localSync(method, model, [options]) {
  if (method == 'get') {
    var json = window.localStorage[model.url],
        data = (json == null) ? {} : JSON.decode(json);
    if (options is Map && options.containsKey('onLoad')) {
      options['onLoad'](data.getValues());
    }
  }
}
```

That is pretty nifty. With a single line, it is possible to inject completely different data syncing behavior for the entire framework.

It is worth pointing out that, because of how Dart manages libraries, setting HipsterSync.sync in one location will change it everywhere. In this case, we set it in our main.dart.

```
// main.dart
import 'HipsterSync.dart';

main() {
  HipsterSync.sync = localSync;
  //
}
```

This will affect the _injected_sync HipsterSync class variable that is seen by Hipster-Model.

```
// HipsterModel.dart
library hipster_model;

import 'HipsterSync.dart';

class HipsterModel {
  // I see HipsterSync._injected_sync from main.dart
}
```

And the same goes, of course, for HipsterCollection.

```
// HipsterCollection.dart
library hipster_collection;
import 'HipsterSync.dart';
class HipsterCollection {
  // I see HipsterSync._injected_sync from main.dart
}
```

Each of these files, main.dart, HipsterModel.dart, HipsterCollection.dart, and HipsterSync.dart, are separate files. And yet Dart ensures that the HipsterSync class defined in one is the same that is seen by all. The only equivalent in JavaScript is what Backbone.js does to define its Backbone.sync. Backbone declares a global variable (for example, Backbone) and instructs developers that it needs to be included via <script> tags before all other code. Using something like require.js will get you close to Dart's behavior, but it is very nice to have this working at the outset of the language rather than attempting to tack it on 18 years after the fact.

What's Next

As mentioned in *Classes and Objects*, Dart frowns on dynamic language features that are necessary for metaprogramming. Even so, it is quite possible to achieve some pretty nifty dynamic language features in Dart. The noSuch-

Method() method is certainly an easy one to hook into for a significant portion of metaprogramming. It is limited to instance methods, but this ought to cover 80 percent of a developer's dynamic programming needs. When that fails, there are still ways to exploit Dart's functional nature to achieve broader dynamic language features. And we have not even mentioned Dart's reflection capabilities, which are already used heavily in projects like Angular.dart.

With a pretty intense code organization project under our collective belt, let's take a look next at something near and dear to anyone who has maintained a large application: testing. If metaprogramming in Dart blew your mind because of the sheer craziness of the topic, testing is going to blow your mind simply by virtue of how great it is.

CHAPTER 12

Testing Dart

As web applications grow in complexity, you can't rely on just type checking to catch bugs. In this chapter, we'll explore testing the Hipster MVC library, which has definitely grown to the too-complex-for-type-checking point.

Obtaining the Test Harness

The unittest library is maintained by the core Dart team, but it is not part of the Dart SDK. Instead, it is hosted on the Dart Pub—the package repository for Dart. The easiest way to install this is to create a pubspec.yaml in the application root directory with contents like the following:

testing/pubspec.yaml
```
name: Dart Comics
dev_dependencies:
  unittest: any
```

The "any" in there refers to any version of the unittest library, which will default to the most recent version. Since unit testing is not needed for the code to run, it is entered as a dev_dependency instead of a regular dependency.

To install package dependencies, run the pub install command from the command line or from the Tools menu of the Dart Editor. By convention, our tests will reside in the test subdirectory of our application.

2 + 2 = 5 Should Be Red

Client-side Dart code must be tested in a running Dart-enabled browser or headless context. A simple web page is required to host the test output. Any old HTML will suffice as long as it does the following:

- Pulls in the Dart tests
- Starts the Dart engine

The dummy test page for testing the HipsterCollection class will be as follows:

```
testing/test/01.html
<html>
<head>
  <title>Hipster Test Suite</title>
  <script type="application/dart"
    src="HipsterCollectionTest.dart"></script>
  <script type="text/javascript">
    navigator.webkitStartDart();      // start Dart
  </script>
</head>

<body>
  <h1>Test!</h1>
</body>
</html>
```

We rely on HipsterCollectionTest.dart to import two required testing libraries as well as our own source code. It also needs to declare the main() entry point since we have not declared it elsewhere.

```
testing/test/HipsterCollectionTest.dart
import 'package:unittest/unittest.dart';
import 'package:unittest/html_enhanced_config.dart';
import "../web/scripts/HipsterCollection.dart" ;
main() {
  useHtmlEnhancedConfiguration();
  // Tests go here!
}
```

In addition to the imports, we invoke useHtmlEnhancedConfiguration(). This will make pretty test results in the browser instead of only printing them in the Dart console. Nothing will happen without a test, however, so let's write one. And in the grand tradition of behavior-driven development, let's start with a failing test.

```
testing/test/02test.dart
import 'package:unittest/unittest.dart';
import 'package:unittest/html_enhanced_config.dart';
import "../web/scripts/HipsterCollection.dart";
main() {
  useHtmlEnhancedConfiguration();

  group('basic', (){
    test('arithmetic', (){
      expect(2 + 2, 5);
    });
  });
}
```

Strictly speaking, a group() method is not required around tests—it just helps organize the output. To try it out, load the HTML in the browser:

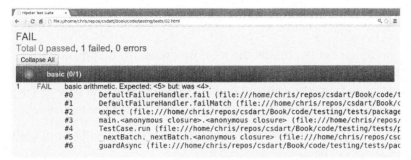

Yay! A failing test! To get the test to pass, we simply need to fix our math.

testing/test/03test.dart
```
group('basic', (){
  test('arithmetic', (){
    expect(2 + 3, 5);
  });
});
```

Reloading the pages produces a green test suite.

Now that you have a basic idea of how to write tests, let's replace our silly arithmetic test with a real test of the HipsterCollection class.

testing/test/04test.dart
```
test('HipsterCollection has multiple models', (){
  HipsterCollection it = new HipsterCollection();
  it.models = [{'id': 17}, {'id': 42}];
  expect(it.length, equals(2));
});
```

This is a simple test of the length getter in our HipsterCollection class. The test() function takes two arguments: a string describing the test and an anonymous function that includes at least one expectation. After a bit of setup, the expectation is checked using Dart's built-in equals() test.

In addition to checking basic equality with the equals test, Dart supports numerous matchers ranging from approximation (closeTo) to basic type checks (isNull, isFalse, isMap). It even supports checking for exceptions. For instance, we can verify that HipsterCollection#fetch() fails without a URL.

testing/test/HipsterCollectionFetch.dart

```
test('HipsterCollection fetch() fails without a url', () {
  var it = new HipsterCollection();
  expect(()=> it.fetch(), throws);
});
```

That is some pretty test code! Inside the test, we create an instance of Hipster-Collection, then use the expect() method to set our expectation—invoking the function that fetches from the collection will throw an error. As new as Dart is, test matchers like throw make it surprisingly powerful and expressive.

We can see some of these testing matchers when we group additional tests that describe aspects of HipsterCollection lookup.

```
group('HipsterCollection lookup', () {
  var model1 = {'id': 17},
      model2 = {'id': 42};

  HipsterCollection it = new HipsterCollection();
  it.models = [model1, model2];

  test('works by ID', () {
    expect(it[17], isNotNull);
    expect(it[17], isMap);
    expect(it[17].values, [17]);
    expect(it[17].keys, equals(['id']));
    expect(it[17], equals(model1));
  });

  test('is null when it does not hold ID', () {
    expect(it[1], isNull);
  });
});
```

Just like that, we have a test suite with three passing tests.

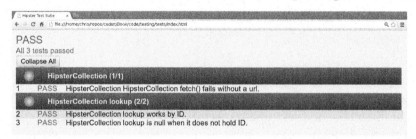

Asynchronous Testing

Dart, like JavaScript, is a functional language. Functional languages present unique challenges to testing. Dart is quite up to that challenge.

Consider, for instance, adding a new element to a HipsterCollection. The expectation in this case is that any listeners for the onAdd events will be invoked with a single argument—the model that was added. The expectation that an asynchronous call will occur is codified in Dart's testing library as expectAsync(). This method takes a function as a parameter—the number of arguments supported by that function describes the arity of expected callback.

To see this in action, we write an asynchronous test that listens for an add event on a HipsterCollection. Instead of a normal event listener, we supply a expectAsync() call. For good measure, we set a separate expectation inside our expectAsync()—that the supplied event is not null.

```
group('Async', (){
  test('HipsterCollection add dispatches insert events', (){
    HipsterCollection it = new HipsterCollection();
    it.onAdd.listen(expectAsync((model) {
      expect(model, isNotNull);
    }));

    it.add({'id': 42});
  });
});
```

Care must be taken with asynchronous tests in Dart. Had we omitted the expectAsync() wrapper, this test would still pass—*even without adding a new record.* The reason for this is that all tests pass unless an expectation does not match. Without the expectAsync() wrapper, this test would pass even if the expect() statement is not executed. The expectAsync() wrapper ensures that the test suite will wait—perhaps indefinitely—until that callback is executed.

With that, we have four reasonably useful tests in place to help catch regressions in our HipsterCollection class.

What's Next

Although still quite new (which is saying something for a language as new as Dart), the unittest library is amazingly powerful. Not only does it support a wealth of testing primitives, but it also supports the sometimes difficult task of callback testing. Although we did not touch on it here, Dart already makes command-line testing easy—meaning simple regression builds. The combination of static type checking and a powerful unit testing library allows the discerning Dart developer to achieve the goal of robust, accurate, maintainable code.

Bearing that in mind, let's spend our last few chapters looking at some of Dart's cooler features.

Part V

The Next Level with Dart

At this point, you have a strong understanding of the power of Dart under your belt. With that, it's time to begin discussing what comes next as Dart evolves. First, we'll remove the last vestiges of JavaScript thinking from Hipster MVC by removing callbacks. Callbacks—long the bane of many a JavaScripter—are replaced with completers, futures, and isolates that promise a simpler way to describe what happens later. Last, we talk about Dart's support for HTML5 and where Dart goes from here.

CHAPTER 13

Project: An End to Callback Hell

One of the knocks on many large JavaScript codebases is the inevitable tangle of callbacks scattered throughout. There is definite power in keeping execution frames small. We need look no further than the rise of Node.js for evidence to support this. But even the most experienced JavaScripters can be confused by the interplay of a myriad of callbacks and events.

So far, our Hipster MVC library exhibits many of the same characteristics of the JavaScript approach—and we have yet to even attempt error handling! As you saw in Chapter 8, *Events and Streams*, on page 77, the syntax for Dart events is different from that of JavaScript, but the approach is very much the same. This is not the case with callbacks. Let's take a look at how the Future class can significantly improve the long-term maintainability of Dart applications.

The Future

When last we saw our HipsterModel, we had replaced direct Ajax calls with a data synchronization layer that was cleverly named HipsterSync. In the save() method, it looks like this:

```
class HipsterModel {

  // ...
  save({callback}) {
    HipsterSync.send('post', this, options: {
      'onLoad': (attrs) {
        attributes = attrs;
        if (callback != null) callback(this);
      }
    });
  }
}
```

There are at least three issues with this approach. First, we are invoking send() with too many arguments—we need to indicate that this is a "post," and this is necessary so that HipsterSync knows what to sync—but the options parameter describes only a side effect and is not needed in order to perform the main execution thread. Second, the readability of the onLoad callback is less than ideal, buried inside the options parameter. Third, it is weak programming practice to null check for the presence of a callback each time we attempt to invoke the callback.

Instead of the callback approach, let's switch to Future objects. In fact, Futures are little more than objects that formalize callbacks. If we switch HipsterSync.send() to return a Future, then we can inject a callback via the then() method.

```
class HipsterModel {
  // ...
  save([callback]) {
    HipsterSync.
      send('post', this).
      then((attrs) {
        attributes = attrs;
        if (callback != null) callback(this);
      });
  // ...
}
```

With that small change, the intention of HipsterSync.send() is much clearer; it does nothing more than POST this (the model) to the back-end data store. Once that is complete, *then* we grab the attributes returned from the data store to do the following:

- Update the model's attributes
- Invoke the callback if it is present

We are in better shape, but there is still the matter of the null check. There are times that a conditional like the one in the then() statement is necessary. More often than not, a null check is our code begging for a better abstraction. This is one of those times.

Instead of an optional callback, we can convert save() to return a Future. The easiest way to generate a Future is by instantiating a new Completer, which has a future getter that can be returned.

```
Future<HipsterModel> save() {
  Completer completer = new Completer();
  // ...
  return completer.future;
}
```

Here, we explicitly state that our Future will return a value of HipsterModel by declaring the return type of save() to be Future<HipsterModel>. That is, upon successful save, save() will send a copy of the current model back to the then() function. For instance, if we wanted to log the ID of a newly created model, we could use the then() function like this:

```
var comic_book = new ComicBook({'title': 'Batman'});
comic_book.
  save().
  then((new_comic) {
    print("I got assigned an ID of ${new_comic['id']}");
  });
```

We still need to tell save() how to actually notify the then() statement in the calling context that anything happened. This is done with the same Completer object that produced the Future. To notify the Future that the Completer has completed, we invoke complete() with the value to be sent to then.

```
class HipsterModel {
  // ...
  Future<HipsterModel> save() {
    Completer completer = new Completer();
    HipsterSync.
      send('post', this).
      then((attrs) {
        this.attributes = attrs;
        completer.complete(this);
      });
    return completer.future;
  }
  // ...
}
```

When HipsterSync.send() successfully completes, then we update the model's attributes and mark save() as complete. By completing the Completer, code that calls save() can then() do what it needs to do. This almost begins to read like English, which is nice.

More importantly, we have significantly improved the readability, and hence the maintainability, of the save() method. We no longer have to worry about an optional callback parameter to save(). Now, invoking send() on HipsterSync involves only the two things needed to effect the requested change (the action to take and the model). There is no more options Map to clutter things. Lastly, by converting this method to a Future itself, we have eliminated a conditional, and in doing so, we have improved life for the caller.

Handling Errors in the Future

Until now, we have conveniently ignored the question of how to handle exceptions. What happens if our POST to the back end results in a 400-class error? How can we design Hipster MVC so that developers can handle exceptions appropriately?

Had we stuck with options, the answer would have been to add yet another callback inside the Map of options. Luckily for us, Completer and Future have a formal mechanism for dealing with just such a situation. A Completer invokes completeError() to signal a problem and Future deals with problems with handleException() to do something with that exception.

The default data sync behavior in HipsterSync would signal an exceptional condition to the future by calling completeError() when the request status is not okay (for example, greater than 299).

```
class HipsterSync {
  // ...
  static Future _defaultSync(method, model) {
    var request = new HttpRequest(),
        completer = new Completer();
    request.
      onLoad.
      listen((event) {
        var req = event.target;
        if (req.status > 299) {
          completer.
            completeError("That ain't gonna work: ${req.status}");
        }

        else {
          var json = JSON.decode(req.responseText);
          completer.complete(json);
        }
      });
    // Open and send the request
    return completer.future;
  }
}
```

The value in completeError does not have to be a subclass of Exception—any old object will do. In this case, we supply a simple string.

```
if (req.status > 299) {
  completer.
    completeError("That ain't gonna work: ${req.status}");
}
```

Back in the model class, we need to handle this exceptional case. The then() method returns void, so it is not chainable. This requires us to store the after-send Future back in HipsterModel.save() in a local variable. We can then inject a happy-path then() behavior into the Future along with handleException() behavior.

```
class HipsterModel {
  // ...
  Future<HipsterModel> save() {
    Completer completer = new Completer();
    Future after_send = HipsterSync.send('post', this);

    after_send.
      then((attrs) { /* ... */ });

    after_send.
      handleException((e) { /* ... */ });
    return completer.future;
  }
}
```

Since HipsterModel#save() is itself a Future, it should handle exceptions with a completeError() of its own.

```
after_send.
  handleException((e) {
    completer.completeError(e);
    return true;
  });
```

What's Next

As you'll see in the next chapter, Futures come in handy in other places. It is easy to see why. Through a very basic application in the Hipster MVC library, we have significantly improved the maintainability of the library as well as made it easier for developers to use the library.

Having built-in objects codifying this behavior is a big win for Dart. It is not hard to build something similar in JavaScript. Even so, built-in Futures allow us to focus on writing beautiful code, not on writing code that allows us to write beautiful code.

CHAPTER 14

Futures and Isolates

In addition to the familiar syntax and concepts that Dart supports, there are a number of higher-level functional programming features that include the likes of completers, futures, and isolates. We have already seen futures a bit in the context of streams, but they are worth touching on by themselves. Futures play a big role in isolates, which use them to facilitate communication between currently executing functions.

Completers and Futures

Completers are objects that encapsulate the idea of finishing a task at some later point. Rather than passing a callback to be invoked along with a future value, Dart allows us to define the entire thing in a completer object.

Since completers trigger an action in the future, completers are intimately tied to Futures. The single most defining characteristic of a Future is a callback function, which is supplied via a Future object's then() method.

In its simplest form, we can create a Completer object and grab the future property from the completer so that we can specify what happens when the completer finishes. Finally, some time later, we tell the completer that it is finished with an optional message.

isolates/simple_completer.dart
```
main() {
  var completer = new Completer();
  var future = completer.future;
  future.then((message) {
    print("Future completed with message: $message");
  });
  completer.complete("foo");
}
```

This prints: Future completed with message: foo

On their own, Futures provide an important but narrow functionality. They do one thing but do it well.

Completers can be completed only once. Trying it twice will throw an error. Here's an example:

`isolates/test/completer.dart`
```
completer.complete("once");
completer.complete("twice");
```

This will produce the following:

```
Future completed with message: foo
Unhandled exception:
Exception: future already completed
```

In addition to sending successful messages from the future, it is possible to signal errors. To support error handling, the Future needs to define a catchError() callback.

`isolates/exceptional_completer.dart`
```
main() {
  var completer = new Completer();
  completer.
    future.
    catchError((e) {
      print("Handled: $e");
      return true;
    });
  var exception = new Exception("Too awesome");
  completer.completeError(exception);
}
```

When the completer completes with an exception, the result is as follows:

```
Handled: Exception: Too awesome
```

Isolates

As the name implies, Dart isolates are used to isolate long-running functions from the main thread of execution. Dart isolates do not share any memory so they rely on message passing for communication, making for very elegant concurrent programming solutions. Message passing is achieved through port objects and uses Futures to signal when isolates and messages are ready.

Isolates are imported from the dart:isolate library. The easiest way to use them is with the Isolate.spawnUri() method.

```
isolates/test/isolates.dart
import 'dart:isolate';

var res = new ReceivePort();
var sender = Isolate.spawnUri(
  Uri.parse('isolates/main.dart'),
  ['2014'],
  res.sendPort
);
sender.
  then((_)=> res.first).
  then((message) {
    print('Doom in 2014 falls on a ${message}.');
  });
```

We will take a look at the main.dart isolate code in a bit. For now, note that the spawnUri() call needs a ReceivePort, which can be passed to the isolate for communication back to the calling context.

Sticking with the calling context, the Isolate.spawnUri() returns a Future, which will complete when the isolate's environment has been constructed. At that point communication between the calling context and the isolate is ready.

To handle the response back from the isolate, we take advantage of a very nice feature of futures in Dart. A then() call that itself returns a Future will complete with the returned future's completion value. Here, we return the first response back on the ReceivePort. It could take several seconds for this long-running calculation to determine the day of doom, so res.first is a future that completes when the first message is sent back. By returning res.first with Dart's hash-rocket return, we pass the response to the next future. In other words, this is a nice way to chain futures.

The semantics end up reading nicely. We spawn an isolate. When the isolate is ready, then we wait for the first response. When the first response comes back, then we print out a nice little message that includes the response.

As for the isolate code itself, it is mercifully free of isolate-related code. It needs a SendPort on which to send its responses, but that is the only suggestion that it is an isolate rather than plain old Dart. Recall that the Isolate.spawnUri() took two parameters besides the location of the script. The first was the list of arguments passed to the isolate. In our case, it was the current year. The second parameter is the first message that we send into the isolate. Our first message was the SendPort property of the ReceivePort that enables the isolate to communicate.

The list of arguments and the "reply to" SendPort become the parameters in the main() entry point of main.dart:

```
main(List<String> args, SendPort replyTo) {
  var year = int.parse(args[0]);
  var doomsday = dayOfDoom(year);
  replyTo.send(doomsday);
}
```

For compatibility, the argument list should be a list of strings, which means that we need to parse the first entry in the list to get the year. After making a call to the super-long-running dayOfDoom() method, we send the response back to the replyTo SendPort.

And that's all there is to the isolate code. There is no need for complex setup or infrastructure to get the benefit of isolated, concurrent programming.

In truth, the doomsday algorithm used in findDoom() is rather simple. It finds the day of the week for the last day in February. With simple mnemonics, we can use that to figure out the day of the week for any day in the year.[1] It makes for a small algorithm that is useful for illustration.

```
final List<String> dayNames = [
  'Mon', 'Tues', 'Wed', 'Thurs', 'Fri', 'Sat', 'Sun'
];

dayOfDoom(year) {
  var march1 = new DateTime(year, 3, 1, 0, 0, 0, 0),
      oneDay = new Duration(days:1),
      date = march1.subtract(oneDay);

  return dayNames[date.weekday - 1];
}
```

Tracing the messages all the way through, the first message is sent from the main context into the spawned isolate via Isolate.spawnUri(). It is the send port through which the isolate can communicate back to the main context. The list of arguments that are sent at the same time can also be considered a message but are typically intended to serve as initialization. Since the isolate does not send back a SendPort of its own, this is the end of communication from the main context into the isolate.

Inside the isolate, the doomsday message is sent back to the calling context on the supplied SendPort. Once that is sent back, the sharing of information between the two contexts is done.

---

1. http://en.wikipedia.org/wiki/Doomsday_rule

The result of calling our doomsday isolate in the following code:

```
var res = new ReceivePort();
var sender = Isolate.spawnUri(
  Uri.parse('isolates/main.dart'),
  ['2014'],
  res.sendPort
);
sender.
  then((_)=> res.first).
  then((message) {
    print('Doom in 2014 falls on a ${message}.');
  });
```

is that 2014's doomsday is a Friday.

```
Doom in 2014 is on a Fri.
```

Beware the Friday.

What's Next

Completers and futures are everywhere in Dart, mostly thanks to streams. They also help out wonderfully when our asynchronous needs grow to the point that separate isolates of code are needed. It is wonderful to know that we do not have to reinvent them or choose the best library available when we need them.

Recent versions of JavaScript include the concept of web workers, but if we need to support older browsers, we are left to our own devices. Early versions of Node.js supported promises, which are quite similar to Futures in Dart. In the end, they were removed from Node.js, leaving the poor hipster to reinvent promises each time the need arises.

Thankfully, in Dart, web workers and promises are supported from the outset in the form of isolates.

Up next, we finish our tour of Dart with a brief look at how the language handles some of the new hotness that browsers have started to support in the last couple of years.

CHAPTER 15

HTML5 and Dart

Back in Chapter 4, *Manipulating the DOM*, on page 29, you saw many examples of how easy Dart makes it to interact and manipulate the DOM and styles. This chapter builds upon basic DOM manipulation to present a guide to adding a little life to web pages through animations, WebSockets, and other sundry techniques that fall under the HTML5 umbrella.

Most of this chapter discusses features that can be accomplished already in JavaScript. What Dart brings to the table is a familiar, simple syntax and cross-platform compatibility (no need for @-webkit and @-moz duplication).

Animation

If you're making interactive, modern websites in 2014 and beyond, a little animation can go a long way. The transition CSS property is one of those small, seemingly innocuous additions that in reality packs in quite a bit of functionality. Consider, for example, the form view from our comic book application. When it's rendered, it might be nice to fade in.

```
import 'dart:html';
import 'dart:async';
import 'HipsterView.dart';
class AddComicForm extends HipsterView {
  // ...
  render() {
    el.style.opacity = '0';
    el.innerHtml = template();
    Timer.run(() {
      el.style
        ..transition = '1s ease-in-out'
        ..opacity = '1';
    }, 1);
  }
}
```

The transition property is the same one from CSS3.[1] It is a space-separated string of individual transition properties describing the following:

- To which styles the transition applies (all, opacity, and so on). In our example, this is not included, so it defaults to all.

- Duration of the animation. Our animation lasts for one second.

- The animation function. There are several available, including ease, ease-in, ease-out, and linear. The ease-in-out function that we use starts slow, accelerates, and then eases into a slow finish.

- The delay before the animation begins. Since we did not include this, the default of no delay (0s) is used.

Tip

Note: When specifying an initial style, a transition, and a finished state, Dart has the habit of "optimizing" away the transition. As a workaround, we place the transition and final state inside a Timer.run() from dart:async. This effectively takes the animation out of the normal synchronous workflow just enough to allow the animation to kick in.

Local Storage

Dart's support for client-side storage is still somewhat unsettled, but as you saw in Chapter 11, *Project: Varying Behavior*, on page 103, it is far enough along that we can already perform localStorage. Although it is synchronous and can be slow, localStorage is the most widely supported client-side storage solution—and the only one currently supported by Dart.

Because it's synchronous (that is, its operations block other activity in client-side applications), it is not well suited for large stores of data. Still, it's quite handy for smaller datasets and prototyping. There is a benefit to its synchronous nature: far less ceremony is involved in using it.

The API for working with localStorage is similar to the traditional JavaScript API—although Dart uses getters and setters instead of the ugly getItem() and setItem() from JavaScript. In both, it is inefficient to store individual objects of a collection separately. Instead, we store serialized JSON representations of Lists or Maps.

```
var json = window.localStorage['Comic Books'],
    comics = (json != null) ? JSON.decode(json) : [];
```

---

1.   https://developer.mozilla.org/en/CSS/-moz-transition

Adding a record to localStorage is a simple matter of updating the deserialized data, reserializing it, and storing the whole thing back in the database.

```
// Oops. We'll fix the spelling in a bit...
comics.push({'id':42, 'title':'Sandmn'});
window.localStorage['Comic Books'] = JSON.encode(comics);
```

This will replace the data that was previously stored in the Comic Books localStorage item.

Updating data in the local store then consists of nothing more than updating the item in the local representation and serializing that back into the data store as JSON.

```
var json = window.localStorage['Comic Books'],
    comics = (json != null) ? JSON.decode(json) : [];

comics.forEach((comic_book) {
  if (comic_book['title'] == 'Sandmn') {
    comic_book['title'] = 'Sandman';
  }
});
window.localStorage['Comic Books'] = JSON.encode(comics);
```

Similarly, deleting is accomplished by removing from the local copy and serializing that back into the localStorage item.

```
var json = window.localStorage['Comic Books'],
    comics = (json != null) ? JSON.decode(json) : [];

awesome_comics.filter((comic_book) {
  return (comic_book['id'] >= 42);
});
window.localStorage['Comic Books'] = JSON.encode(comics);
```

It doesn't get much easier than localStorage. Unfortunately, each of those operations blocks the browser from doing anything else. So, if our application has too much data on the browser, then it's time to consider something with a little more power.

> **Tip**
>
> Important: At the time of this writing, the APIs for both IndexedDB and Web SQL were not ready for regular usage. Ideally, this will change in time for a future edition of this book.

WebSockets

WebSockets is a wonderful new technology that allows for truly asynchronous communication between the browser and the server. No longer are web developers relegated to awkward hacks like comet or Ajax long-polling. The browser can now open a websocket to the server and push data over that open connection on demand. Better still, when the server has new information available, it can push it immediately to the user over that same websocket.

Dart's support for WebSockets is quite nice. This makes it nearly trivial to, for example, swap out the data syncing layer in our comic book app to use WebSockets instead of Ajax.

```dart
import 'dart:html';
import 'HipsterSync.dart';
// Library scope so that both main() and wsSync()
// have access to the same websocket
WebSocket ws;
main() {
  HipsterSync.sync = wsSync;
  ws = new WebSocket("ws://localhost:3000/");

  // Don't fetch until the websocket is open so
  // that wsSync can talk over an active
  // websocket
  ws.
    onOpen.
    listen((_) {
      var my_comics_collection = new Collections.Comics()
      my_comics_collection.fetch();
      // other initialization...
    });
}
```

We create websocket objects by instantiating the WebSocket constructor with a proper ws:// websocket URL. Websockets are completely asynchronous, which includes opening the connection. Therefore, we add a listener for the websocket's open event. When the connection is open, we can start performing data synchronization operations such as fetching the data over the websocket.

> **Tip**　Note: As of this writing, Dart does not support declaring subprotocols for websockets.

Sending messages over websockets is trivial—we need only invoke ws.send(message). Recall that the data sync method in HipsterSync needs to accept two arguments: the CRUD method and the model (or collection) being synced.

Using that information, we can craft a message to be sent over a websocket to the back end.

```
wsSync(method, model) {
  String message = "$method: ${model.url}";
  if (method == 'delete')
    message = "$method: ${model.id}";
  if (method == 'create')
    message = "$method: ${JSON.encode(model.attributes)}";
  ws.send(message);
}
```

That will send the message, but we need to handle a response from the server and, in turn, inform the rest of the stack of the response. As you saw in Chapter 13, *Project: An End to Callback Hell*, on page 121, informing the Hipster-Sync class is done with a Future. So, our wsSync layer needs its own Completer object, and it needs to complete once the response has been received from the server.

```
wsSync(method, model) {
  final completer = new Completer();
  String message = /* determine the message */
  ws.send(message);
  ws.
    onMessage.
    listen(_wsHandler(event) {
      completer.
        complete(JSON.decode(event.data));
      event.target.on.message.remove(_wsHandler);
    });
  return completer.future;
}
```

The return value of our sync function is a Future. HipsterSync expects this and, in turn, has a corresponding then() clause to propagate this information throughout the Hipster MVC stack once the completer has been marked as finished. Upon receipt of the server response inside the message handler, we complete the Future with the message from the server, which is available in the message event's data attribute.

In this case, we want to listen only for a single response from the server, so we remove the handler after the completer is finished. If this message handler had been left in place, it would continue to receive messages upon the second response from the server (for example, in response to a user-initiated create). Since the completer referenced inside this sync closure has already been terminated, the application would generate all sorts of messages about already completed completers.

Websockets in Dart are really no more difficult or easier than their counterpart in JavaScript. Still, there is a uniquely Darty take on it, which makes them a pleasure to use.

Canvas

Dart lacks something like Raphaël.js[2] that eases some of the pain associated with working with the <canvas> element. Even so, it brings its own Darty take on the staple of HTML5 games everywhere.

As with traditional canvas, Dart still requires a <canvas> element and a corresponding drawing context. If the page already has a <canvas> element, we obtain a drawing context with the getContext() method.

```
CanvasElement canvas = document.query('canvas');
CanvasRenderingContext2D context = canvas.getContext('2d');
```

Given the context, we can draw all sorts of wonderful things. For example, we can draw an empty, white rectangle on the entire canvas as a backdrop.

```
int width = context.canvas.width, height = context.canvas.height;
// start drawing
context.beginPath();
// clear drawing area
context.clearRect(0,0,width,height);
context.fillStyle = 'white';
context.fillRect(0,0,width,height);
// done drawing
context.closePath();
```

A plain white background is not terribly interesting. To spice it up a little, we can add a simple red square that will represent our current location in a game room. If our current location is encapsulated by a Player object that has an x and a y position, then our initial placement might look something like this:

```
// start drawing
context.beginPath();
// clear drawing area
// ...
// draw me
context.rect(me.x, me.y, 20, 20);
context.fillStyle = 'red';
context.fill();
context.strokeStyle = 'black';
context.stroke();
// done drawing
context.closePath();
```

---

2.   http://raphaeljs.com/

That draws a 20 pixel square representing me, filled with red and with a black border. Now all that's needed is a document listener to handle arrow key presses. When an arrow key is pressed, the event moves the player by calling move() in the appropriate direction and then redrawing the entire canvas.

```
document.
  on.
  keyDown.
  add((event) {
    String direction;

    // Listen for arrow keys
    if (event.keyCode == 37) direction = 'left';
    if (event.keyCode == 38) direction = 'up';
    if (event.keyCode == 39) direction = 'right';
    if (event.keyCode == 40) direction = 'down';
    if (direction != null) {
      event.preventDefault();
      me.move(direction);
      draw(me, context);
    }
  });
```

Here, the draw() function performs the same context manipulation that we did previously, only with an updated position for me.

As Dart evolves, no doubt there will be more improvements to the API to make it a little easier to work with. More importantly, there ought to be many libraries built on top of it. Already there is an early port of the Box2D library into Dart that can draw simple physics. Aptly named DartBox2D,[3] it is well worth checking out.

Wrapping Up

This was rather a grab bag of various tools currently available to the Dart developer. But really, that's what HTML5 is—a grab bag of techniques available in newer browsers. They are techniques handled with aplomb by Dart. Perhaps by the time that the 2.0 edition of this book is ready, each of these sections can be broken out into their own chapters. As good as it is now, it is only going to improve as Dart itself continues to evolve.

And Dart is going to evolve. Dramatically. Nearly 100 people are dedicated full-time to improving the language. More importantly, the community that has sprung up around Dart is extremely active. So, please, join us at https://groups.google.com/a/dartlang.org/group/misc/topics, and add your voice!

---

3.   http://code.google.com/p/dartbox2d/

Index

The Modern Web

Get up to speed on the latest HTML, CSS, and JavaScript techniques.

HTML5 and CSS3 (2nd edition)

HTML5 and CSS3 are more than just buzzwords—
they're the foundation for today's web applications.
This book gets you up to speed on the HTML5 elements
and CSS3 features you can use right now in your current projects, with backwards compatible solutions
that ensure that you don't leave users of older browsers
behind. This new edition covers even more new features, including CSS animations, IndexedDB, and
client-side validations.

Brian P. Hogan
(300 pages) ISBN: 9781937785598. $38
http://pragprog.com/book/bhh52e

Async JavaScript

With the advent of HTML5, front-end MVC, and
Node.js, JavaScript is ubiquitous—and still messy.
This book will give you a solid foundation for managing
async tasks without losing your sanity in a tangle of
callbacks. It's a fast-paced guide to the most essential
techniques for dealing with async behavior, including
PubSub, evented models, and Promises. With these
tricks up your sleeve, you'll be better prepared to
manage the complexity of large web apps and deliver
responsive code.

Trevor Burnham
(104 pages) ISBN: 9781937785277. $17
http://pragprog.com/book/tbajs

Seven in Seven

From Web Frameworks to Concurrency Models, see what the rest of the world is doing with this introduction to seven different approaches.

Seven Web Frameworks in Seven Weeks

Whether you need a new tool or just inspiration, *Seven Web Frameworks in Seven Weeks* explores modern options, giving you a taste of each with ideas that will help you create better apps. You'll see frameworks that leverage modern programming languages, employ unique architectures, live client-side instead of server-side, or embrace type systems. You'll see everything from familiar Ruby and JavaScript to the more exotic Erlang, Haskell, and Clojure.

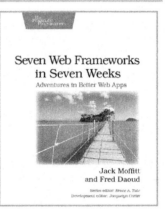

Jack Moffitt, Fred Daoud
(302 pages) ISBN: 9781937785635. $38
http://pragprog.com/book/7web

Seven Concurrency Models in Seven Weeks

Your software needs to leverage multiple cores, handle thousands of users and terabytes of data, and continue working in the face of both hardware and software failure. Concurrency and parallelism are the keys, and *Seven Concurrency Models in Seven Weeks* equips you for this new world. See how emerging technologies such as actors and functional programming address issues with traditional threads and locks development. Learn how to exploit the parallelism in your computer's GPU and leverage clusters of machines with MapReduce and Stream Processing. And do it all with the confidence that comes from using tools that help you write crystal clear, high-quality code.

Paul Butcher
(296 pages) ISBN: 9781937785659. $38
http://pragprog.com/book/pb7con

Put the "Fun" in Functional

Elixir puts the "fun" back into functional programming, on top of the robust, battle-tested, industrial-strength environment of Erlang.

Programming Elixir

You want to explore functional programming, but are put off by the academic feel (tell me about monads just one more time). You know you need concurrent applications, but also know these are almost impossible to get right. Meet Elixir, a functional, concurrent language built on the rock-solid Erlang VM. Elixir's pragmatic syntax and built-in support for metaprogramming will make you productive and keep you interested for the long haul. This book is *the* introduction to Elixir for experienced programmers.

Dave Thomas
(240 pages) ISBN: 9781937785581. $36
http://pragprog.com/book/elixir

Programming Erlang (2nd edition)

A multi-user game, web site, cloud application, or networked database can have thousands of users all interacting at the same time. You need a powerful, industrial-strength tool to handle the really hard problems inherent in parallel, concurrent environments. You need Erlang. In this second edition of the best-selling *Programming Erlang*, you'll learn how to write parallel programs that scale effortlessly on multicore systems.

Joe Armstrong
(548 pages) ISBN: 9781937785536. $42
http://pragprog.com/book/jaerlang2

The Pragmatic Bookshelf

The Pragmatic Bookshelf features books written by developers for developers. The titles continue the well-known Pragmatic Programmer style and continue to garner awards and rave reviews. As development gets more and more difficult, the Pragmatic Programmers will be there with more titles and products to help you stay on top of your game.

Visit Us Online

This Book's Home Page
http://pragprog.com/book/csdart1
Source code from this book, errata, and other resources. Come give us feedback, too!

Register for Updates
http://pragprog.com/updates
Be notified when updates and new books become available.

Join the Community
http://pragprog.com/community
Read our weblogs, join our online discussions, participate in our mailing list, interact with our wiki, and benefit from the experience of other Pragmatic Programmers.

New and Noteworthy
http://pragprog.com/news
Check out the latest pragmatic developments, new titles and other offerings.

Save on the eBook

Save on the eBook versions of this title. Owning the paper version of this book entitles you to purchase the electronic versions at a terrific discount.

PDFs are great for carrying around on your laptop—they are hyperlinked, have color, and are fully searchable. Most titles are also available for the iPhone and iPod touch, Amazon Kindle, and other popular e-book readers.

Buy now at *http://pragprog.com/coupon*

Contact Us

Online Orders:	*http://pragprog.com/catalog*
Customer Service:	*support@pragprog.com*
International Rights:	*translations@pragprog.com*
Academic Use:	*academic@pragprog.com*
Write for Us:	*http://write-for-us.pragprog.com*
Or Call:	+1 800-699-7764

CPSIA information can be obtained at www.ICGtesting.com
Printed in the USA
BVOW09s1301010315

389666BV00005B/10/P